Palgrave Studies in Race, Inequality and Social Justice in Education

Series Editor
Dave S.P. Thomas, Solent University, Aylesford, UK

This series focuses on new developments in the study of race, social justice and education. Promoting theoretically-rich works, contributions include empirical and conceptual studies that advance critical analysis whilst attempting to destabilise the institutionalised racist orthodoxy that has undermined the notion of education being a tool of social mobility. The series will consider social mobility as a form of equality narrowly defined whilst also critiquing the ideology of social mobility which essentially pits individuals against one another in a sink or swim competition, entirely ignoring the reality of deep and damaging structural inequalities. A central aim of the series will be to address important current policy issues, such as social mobility, widening participation etc., while also recognising that critical studies of race are also concerned with wider, fundamental transformations in education, knowledge and society, i.e. the dismantling of racist structures, concern with education's role in reproducing racial inequality.

Tyler Denmead · Amina Shareef

Rethinking Critical Race Theory

Education Against Elimination in a Time of Genocide

Tyler Denmead (iD)
Faculty of Education
University of Cambridge
Cambridge, UK

Amina Shareef (iD)
Faculty of Education
University of Cambridge
Cambridge, UK

ISSN 2524-633X   ISSN 2524-6348 (electronic)
Palgrave Studies in Race, Inequality and Social Justice in Education
ISBN 978-3-032-07748-6   ISBN 978-3-032-07749-3 (eBook)
https://doi.org/10.1007/978-3-032-07749-3

This work was supported by University of Cambridge.

Cover illustration: © Melisa Hasan

This Palgrave Macmillan imprint is published by the registered company Springer Nature Switzerland AG
The registered company address is: Gewerbestrasse 11, 6330 Cham, Switzerland

If disposing of this product, please recycle the paper.

CONTENTS

CHAPTER 1

Introduction

Abstract Critical race theory has been the dominant educational theory for understanding how 'race' and racism are reproduced and contested in education. However, the tenets of critical race theory were developed to understand and challenge how 'race' and racism operate within the context of the United States. And while critical race theory has been translated for educational contexts in other nations, there remains a pressing need to develop a more global orientation to critical race theory. As decolonial scholars have pointed out, 'race' and racism are endemic and deeply constitutive of modernity. Taking a global and historical approach, we address the ways in which educational systems throughout the world reproduce-and contest-a global system marked, not only by racial discrimination, segregation, and exclusion, but also by racialised death and elimination.

Keywords Social Theories · Educational Theories · Global Approach · Critical Race Theory · Race · Racism · Decolonization

During the 2023–24 academic year, pro-Palestine protests erupted on college and university campuses in more than 25 countries. These protests objected to Israel's ongoing military operation in the occupied West Bank and its genocide of Palestinian people in the occupied Gaza Strip.

© The Author(s) 2026   1
T. Denmead and A. Shareef, *Rethinking Critical Race Theory*, Palgrave
Studies in Race, Inequality and Social Justice in Education,
https://doi.org/10.1007/978-3-032-07749-3_1

Between 7 October 2023, the date of the Hamas attacks on Israel, and April 2025, modest estimates suggest that 52,000 Palestinians, or 2.5% of its population, were killed. Forced displacement had resulted in a population decline of 6 per cent. By May 2025, 80% of the schools and universities in Gaza were destroyed or damaged, with all its 12 universities demolished. Various international organisations, including Human Rights Watch, accused Israel of using starvation as a weapon of war. The vast majority of those displaced, starved, maimed, and killed were Muslim. In response, protestors on college and university campuses around the world set up encampments, occupied buildings, staged walkouts, and organised teach-ins. These protests called attention to the mass killing, depopulation, and near-complete destruction of Gaza's life-critical infrastructure–including its educational system. Identifying the genocidal intent of the Israeli settler colonial regime, protestors turned on their universities and demanded they disclose financial ties to Israel, divest from partnerships with Israeli institutions, and provide amnesty to protestors in university disciplinary procedures. In return, protestors were criticised for making unrealistic demands, spreading anti-Semitic views, interfering with university life, and undermining Israel's right to exist and defend itself. Their social media accounts were shadow banned, their personal information was doxxed, and their reputations were smeared.

In the weeks and months following the inauguration of Donald Trump as United States (US) president in January 2025, the US federal government began targeting universities, particularly those belonging to the elite 'Ivy League' located on the East Coast. Harvard University, the most prestigious university in the country, was targeted as a part of a broader campaign to intimidate and weaken all American institutions of higher learning. Trump's Vice-President J.D. Vance was one of the key architects of this campaign. Vance once said that the American political right should 'seize the institutions of the left and turn them against the left. We need ... a de-Baathification programme, a de-woke-ification programme' (Pogue 2022). By linking an Arab nationalist and socialist ideology with 'institutions of the left,' including universities, Vance used a global racial grammar to position American higher education as a hostile internal enemy of Western, White, and American interests. In the wake of these pro-Palestine protests, the federal attack on this internal enemy included defunding scientific research, rolling back admissions and staffing practices designed to redress histories of discrimination, revoking international student visas for political speech, and ceasing to process international student visas. Perhaps most terrifyingly, un-uniformed federal security officials seized several Muslim international students on American university campuses who had participated in these protests. These students were held in immigration detention centres and then processed for deportation.

This political aim to 'seize the institutions of the left and turn them against the left' has been driven in part by the belief that modern leftism focuses too much on 'race' and racism. From this vantage point, modern leftism suffers from an affliction of critical race theory. This affliction manifests when liberals use racism as a cudgel to punish people, particularly White people. This political narrative has been key to the rise of Trumpism. After all, Trumpism is driven in some measure by White resentment, if not rage, over perceived White losses in both cultural and economic terms (Hooker 2017), and even losses at the population level—what is known as 'White genocide conspiracy theory' (see Davis 2025). The curriculum in schools and universities has yet again become a battlefield on which White loss is to be reversed and White supremacy is to be restored. This political movement blames critical race theory for pushing out White authors who have dominated curricula for decades and replacing them with Black, Indigenous, Asian, and Muslim authors. Schools are denounced for making White students feel shame and guilt for long-gone racist pasts for which they are not responsible, such as plantation slavery and settler colonialism. From this perspective, White people are now victims of racism, facilitated by affirmative action, reverse discrimination, anti-racist and multicultural education, liberal immigration policies, and do-good humanitarianism.

Against this social and political backdrop, pro-Palestine protestors were criticised for overstating the significance of 'race' and racism in their analysis of the genocide in occupied Gaza. David Leonhardt, the editorial director for *New York Times* opinion section, spelled out this criticism. 'There is a version of modern leftism that sees almost everything through the prism of race,' he stated. 'So, Israel has become particularly important because, in this version of leftism, it is a story of White people oppressing dark-skinned people...' (Leonhardt et al. 2025). Leonhardt then suggested that a growing number of Black, Latino, and Asian voters in the US had rejected modern leftism's focus on 'race' and racism when they turned to support Trumpism in the 2024 elections (Leonhardt et al. 2025). If Black, Latino, and Asian voters in the US have opposed this brand of modern leftism, then, this argument holds, 'race' and racism as a global analytical framework is a gross political miscalculation, if not a grave analytical error.

In this book, we strongly oppose this view. A global critical race perspective is necessary analytically irrespective of its effectiveness in electoral politics. It is necessary for educationists to explain how educational systems and practices in one part of the world are implicated in the production of racial valuation and colonial violence in another part of the world. It is necessary for educationists to explain how educational systems and practices in different national contexts draw down from the same forms of racism, such as anti-Muslim racism, that circulate globally. And crucially, a global critical race perspective is necessary to create educational systems and practices that produce worlds that are not predicated on the death of those who are targeted as racially inferior and historically immature. A global critical race perspective is needed to advance educational projects that are against the elimination of people based on their ascribed inferiority and their chosen ways of life.

We began writing this book to address these theoretical and practical concerns as the genocide in occupied Gaza has unfolded. As we observe this livestreamed genocide from our phones, we could not help but ask one question: why has the Palestinian cause garnered so much support across the globe in various sites such as university campuses and broadcast media. After all, there are other political projects unfolding as we write this book that threaten the life of Muslim populations in places such as India, China, Myanmar, and Kashmir. Asking this same question at the Critical Muslim Studies Conference in Istanbul in June 2025 was Professor Salman Sayyid, one of the key figures in the development of a post-Orientalist decolonial study of the Islamicate. He, too, observed that the plight of Muslims in these territories has not accumulated the same level of attention or solidarity as the elimination of life, and ways of life, in the occupied territories of Palestine. Collectively, we struggle to understand why.

Our reflections bring us to the following explanation: Occupied Palestine brings to the surface the subterranean structures of race and racism that are the enduring foundations of the modern world, foundations that are too easily concealed and denied. Colonial dominance over racially inferiorised and subordinated people—involving the relentless threat of humiliation and death—is an inexpugnable feature of the modern world, not an aberration of history. The control and elimination of Palestinians in occupied territories exposes the racial dividing line that justifies who deserves and does not deserve to die in the modern world. This genocide thus clearly distils the dividing lines in a long history of racial-colonial violence, making it an obvious target for political protest and contestation. Indeed, W.E.B. Du Bois (2008) famously stated that the problem of the world we have inherited is *the color line*. With this concept, Du Bois made it clear that this global and historical cut between 'darker' and 'lighter' populations produces a global system of racial power in what he called *The White World* (Du Bois 1940). From this point of view, the 'lighter races' throughout the world develop a collective interest to protect their advantages and dominate 'darker races.' This ugly truth of The White World is on display in Palestine.

This racial dividing line based on colour is not clearly obvious in other places where Brown/Muslim populations face elimination by state violence. Racial projects in India, Kashmir, Western China, and Myanmar take place between 'dark-skinned' people (Hindu Indians, Han Chinese, and Buddhist Burmese) and other 'dark-skinned' people (Muslim Kashmiris, Muslim Uyghurs, and Muslim Rohingyas). At first glance, these deathly projects seem neither related to the unfolding genocide in the Gaza strip nor racial/colonial in character. However, it is possible to see this dimension if we recognise that, while colour has been an important way in which people have been racialised and positioned within systems of racial power, it is not the exclusive signifier of 'race'. Indeed, culture, nationality, language, religion, people's names, and even clothing have all contributed symbolically to processes of racialisation throughout the history of the modern world. In this way, Muslim Kashmiris, Uyghurs, and Rohingyas are being racialised when they are being targeted with state violence that casts them as a cultural and populational threat to the purity of nations.

Since the beginning of the modern age in the long sixteenth century, if not earlier, the West has identified a singular—and linear—pathway that racialised populations must take on their journey to becoming modern. This pathway requires populations to strip themselves and their nations from their Nativeness, Jewishness, Muslimness, Blackness, and Asianness. According to this logic, the modernisation of populations deemed to lack White European rationality is only possible through the imitation or adoption of White European values, beliefs, norms, standards, and practices. This process of *assimilation,* or perhaps more provocatively framed as *deracialisation,* takes place through education in both subtle and terrifyingly violent ways, from the White curriculum to colonial residential schools (Goldberg 2002, 83). This process of modernisation often takes the population as its object through racial projects of re-education, amalgamation, expulsion, and outright killing. This logic of modernisation means that the use of violence is necessary, especially against resistance to forced Westernisation (Dussel 2000, 472). To paraphrase the Cameroonian decolonial thinker, Achille Mbembe, the destruction of people's ways of life is touted as necessary to save people from themselves for the betterment of humanity (Mbembe 2003, 22; see footnote 38). Crucially, what has been at stake in this global racial and colonial struggle throughout the history of the modern world is the elimination of people and their ways of life.

From this long historical and global perspective, it becomes easier to see why we should be paying just as much attention to the threat of elimination against Muslims in India, Kashmir, Western China, and Myanmar as the unfolding genocide in Gaza. Or, to put it another way, state-sanctioned elimination of Muslim life, and ways of life, is interconnected across multiple locations. What is common across these political projects is a single world-shaping telos and trajectory: modernisation seeks to regulate, expel, and eliminate racialised inferiority and historical immaturity. Today, Muslimness is one of the important signifiers of racial inferiority, primitiveness, and barbarity. The interconnectedness of these eliminatory projects should therefore be at the centre of our concerns as critical educationists. Their connection alerts us to the fact that people throughout the world learn that this regulation, expulsion, and elimination of racialised inferiority and historical immaturity is a natural and legitimate, if not necessary, pathway for populations and nations to follow. For many, modernisation is a poisoned chalice, where the death of difference is exchanged for a chance to flourish and avoid being banished to what Achille Mbembe (2003, 40) calls *death-worlds*—or, those living conditions that are more akin to dying than living. Critically, education is a vital mechanism in modernisation in the shape of westernisation that reproduces White domination. The reproduction of The White World continues to promise death and destruction for racially inferiorised and primitivised populations.

Our choice of elimination as a key term used in this book may seem hyperbolic. Indeed, it is not a term commonly used in critical educational thought. As far as we are aware, no one has called for an education against elimination although David Wallace Adams (1995) illuminated how *education for extinction* is a settler colonial project. The tendency in critical education has been to mobilise educational systems and practices to resist *oppression*—not elimination. Indeed, the most important work in the history of critical pedagogy, Paulo Freire's *Pedagogy of the Oppressed* (2000), uses this vocabulary of *oppression*. Oppression refers to the unjust exercise of power over subjugated groups. Another major influence on critical educational thought has been Michel Foucault's (1976) concept of *disciplining*. Disciplining refers to the subtle shaping of people's bodies and behaviour around a set of dominant norms at the expense of those who do not follow them. Today, critical education studies have also been drawn towards challenging both *colonisation* and *coloniality* in education. Colonisation persists in settler colonial contexts whereas coloniality refers to colonial relations of power and knowledge that endure long after the formal end of colonial rule. Since the *Rhodes Must Fall* movement in South Africa in 2015, *decolonizing the curriculum* has become the term du jour in critical education thought. For those in settler colonial contexts, this term, decolonise, can be used too metaphorically and ambiguously. Indeed, the review of educational literature that employs the term decolonise indicates as much (see Shahjahan et al. 2022). Critical Indigenous and decolonial scholars Eve Tuck and K. Wayne Yang (2012) remind us that decolonisation in education should be unsettling because it 'brings about the repatriation of Indigenous land and life,' 'not a metaphor for other things we want to do to improve our societies and schools' (1). Decolonisation has even been co-opted by Far-Right movements in contexts such as the US and India to legitimise deportation and state violence against immigrants and Muslim people constructed as an illegal and invading force (see Davidson 2024; Kliemann 2023). While these concepts outlined above are significant and powerful in any critical educational analysis, including our own, these terms do not speak effectively to the long history of The White World and its irrational desire to eliminate racialised and colonised populations and their ways of life through violence. We must therefore work towards developing educational systems and practices that are against elimination. This imperative has been made crystal clear through the unleashing of death in Gaza and its relationship to racial and colonial violence in other transnational contexts. The global stakes for critical education are nothing short of life saving.

The concept of elimination has particular significance in critical Indigenous studies. It is most often associated with Patrick Wolfe's (2006) articulation of the logic underpinning settler colonialism. Wolfe argued that settler colonial power both necessitates and produces the destruction of Indigenous peoples and their societies. For Wolfe, Indigenous people are made into 'Natives' when they are targeted for their land. The aim of settler colonial power is to acquire and expatriate Indigenous people from this land and replace its former polity with that of the settlers. This aim, according to Wolfe, leads to genocidal acts of forced assimilation, expulsion, and killing. Wolfe's logic of elimination has been debated in critical Indigenous studies. This framing of this logic suggests that the elimination of Indigenous people and their ways of life might not have happened, or might not continue to happen, if not for the motive to steal land.

Yet the gruesome massacre of populations targeted as 'Natives' both in the past and in the present seems to suggest a necropolitical impulse that exceeds this motive for land. The violence we have witnessed suggests an irrational desire to eliminate people and their ways of life who are deemed a threat to Western modernity. This orientation to elimination is expressed in the *necropolitical* view of modern power (Mbembe 2003). The Cameroonian decolonial thinker, Achille Mbembe (2003), argued that one way social and political power is exercised in Western modernity is by exercising 'the will and the capacity to kill in order to live' (18). In other words, people and their nations gain vitality and strength by exercising their power to eliminate people and their ways of life. The necropolitical dividing line between those who get to live and those who are made to die is 'race'. A necropolitical view of elimination thus beckons educationists to radically test the possibilities and promises of education, to do much more than resist oppression, counter the normalisation of dominant expressions of life, or risk using decolonisation metaphorically or even violently. Education needs strategies that imagine worlds free from the Western and White desire to eliminate those marked with racial inferiority, historical immaturity, and global periphery.

Since the mid-1990s, the dominant framework for interrogating the role of education in reproducing systems structured in racial dominance has been critical race theory (Ladson-Billings and Tate IV 1995). Indeed, as Americans who have studied and practised education from a critical vantage point, our first introduction to the study of 'race' and racism was through this framework. This framework emerged in the 1990s in the US to explain how its educational systems, institutions, and practices maintain existing patterns of dominance and subordination between racial groups long after the elimination of legally sanctioned racial discrimination in the 1960s. Contrary to popular misconceptions, the aim of critical race theory in education has never been to develop educational strategies that help individuals overcome their private racist beliefs. Indeed, critical race theory has long held the view that patterns of racial dominance are reproduced by and large without individuals harbouring explicit racial prejudice or displaying overt racism. As a result, critical race theory has called for mobilising educational mechanisms to disrupt the reproduction of the racial status quo irrespective of individual or group intentions. In so doing, it has highlighted key mechanisms by which racial hierarchies are sustained. These mechanisms include:

1. Excluding certain racial groups from educational systems and schools.
2. Segregating certain racial groups within educational systems and schools.
3. Providing racial groups access to different quality educational systems and schools.
4. Creating different experiences for racial groups within the same educational systems and schools.
5. Teaching knowledge that makes racist outcomes appear natural and legitimate.
6. Ignoring knowledge that calls into question the naturalness and legitimacy of those racist outcomes.
7. Cultivating emotions that make racial patterns feel natural and legitimate.
8. Discrediting emotions that unsettle the naturalness and legitimacy of these racial patterns.
9. Bestowing different levels of social, cultural, political, and economic rewards to racial groups from the same educational systems and schools; and,
10. Bestowing different levels of social, cultural, political, and economic rewards to educational institutions based on their racial associations.

This complex array of educational mechanisms often exists in tandem, thus enabling dominant racial groups to leverage education to maintain their position of power, prestige, and reward within a social system structured through 'race'.

In the early 2000s, critical race theory in education inspired education scholars to explain how these mechanisms of racial power operate in education through intersections with other aspects of an individual's social identity, including heritage, language, citizenship, sex, gender, sexual orientation, class, and disability. This 'second wave' led to the creation of various offshoots of critical race theory in education, which we will discuss later in this book. And it led to the translation and adaption of critical race theory to other national educational contexts—including the context where we now teach and study, the United Kingdom (UK). The exportation of critical race theory in education to other national contexts demonstrates that the key tenets of critical race theory—including that racism is a permanent and endemic feature of the modern nation-state—is a useful analytic for explaining racism as it manifests in various sites around the world. Despite this success, critical race theory has been criticised by education scholars and students outside the US-context for several reasons. Its origins as a critique of American society and its educational systems, as well as its initial focus on the White-Black racial binary, can mean that this perspective seems unhelpful for explaining the racial histories and race relations between social groups who are neither racialised as White nor Black in other national contexts. For this reason, critically oriented education scholars and students have thus been turning to decolonial perspectives, particularly from Latin American and Caribbean contexts, which offer a transnational and historical perspective on 'race' and racism that critical race theory has often not provided. Decolonial perspectives have also been more explicit in recognising that the problem of 'race' and racism in education is not merely discrimination and oppression. The problem is also the elimination of people and their ways of life.

Despite these criticisms, we hold on to the belief that critical race theory nonetheless offers a powerful framework for explaining the work of racial projects in education at local, national, and global scales. Critical race theory draws attention to how education operates at the national level to reproduce and maintain structural racial advantages and disadvantages. What has been missing from this perspective, however, has been a transnational orientation that seeks to draw connections between these national projects across the world. What has also been missing is a consideration of what is at stake with 'race' in education in terms that go beyond discrimination and oppression. The need for a global orientation to critical race theory that calls attention to the biopolitical stakes of elimination is necessary now. This urgency became clear to us as we sought to establish links between the crackdown on pro-Palestinian protestors on university campuses in the US and the destruction of Palestinian schools and libraries, the killing of Palestinian teachers and students in occupied Gaza and their relationship to state violence against Muslims in other contexts. While we have written this book particularly mindful of an absence of literature on anti-Muslim racism in critical race theory education scholarship, we believe this perspective remains relevant to those seeking to understand other global forms of racism. We hope this book is therefore useful for a wide audience of students and scholars who are seeking to engage in a multi-scalar and transnational educational analysis of 'race' and racism in the modern world.

* * *

In writing this book, we are conscious that its readers may have only heard the term 'critical race theory' in the contemporary culture wars, particularly in the US and the UK. We use scare quotes here because the 'critical race theory' of the culture wars is not the same as critical race theory of the academy. Instead, 'critical race theory' is now often uttered lazily in non-academic contexts to refer to almost any effort that seeks to combat racism in society, from unconscious bias training in workplaces to school curriculum that teaches the history of transatlantic slavery. The key architect of this attack on 'critical race theory', Christopher Rufo, chose this term to frame the right's attack on modern leftism because it is easier for the right to attack 'critical race theory' than anti-racism (Douthat 2025). Anti-racism has been one of the key vocabularies of modern leftism (see Kendi 2019). But attacking anti-racism positions the attacker as pro-racism, thus minimising the effectiveness of the political attack. So, Rufo chose the term 'critical race theory' to mobilise a movement against modern leftism and its focus on 'race' and racism.

David Theo Goldberg (2023), a preeminent scholar of critical race theory, has done important work on 'critical race theory' in the culture wars. This assault on 'critical race theory' is shaped by the racial ideology of *color-blind racism* (see Fig. 1.1). This racial ideology states that policies and practices in all spheres of liberal life, including educational contexts, must treat everyone equally (and therefore not 'see' race). This racial ideology protects White interests and advantages through casting any effort to address racial disadvantages as racist (see Bonilla-Silva 2010). Following this script, The Heritage Foundation, an American conservative think tank, has compiled steps that people can follow to stop the spread of 'critical race theory' because 'critical race theory' itself, according to this logic, produces racist outcomes against primarily White people ('How to Identify Critical Race Theory', n.d.). In the US context, Asian people are often positioned as victims of this reverse discrimination as well to cast doubt on the view that the attack on 'critical race theory' is a cynical attempt to protect White interests. One step, Heritage advises, is to look for the word 'equity' rather than 'equality' in educational policies and programmes because, as their guidance states, an equity initiative 'demands race-based discrimination' to 'forcibly produce equal outcomes' ('How to Identify Critical Race Theory', n.d.). In this upside-down reality, 'critical race theory' perpetuates racial discrimination against racially dominant people.

Our main interest in this attack on 'critical race theory' is its transnational implications. Attacking 'critical race theory' is not only a means to protect, say, White interests within the nation, but also a way to chill criticism that threatens White interests outside the nation. Moreover, we write this book recognising that these disingenuous attacks on 'critical race theory' both within and beyond the US have produced gross misunderstandings of the school of thought known as critical race theory. These attacks have made it difficult to engage with good-faithed criticisms of this framework. For those who think with this framework, it is natural to feel an impulse to defend this perspective amidst these bad-faith attacks. Nonetheless, it is crucial that we continue to rethink this powerful framework considering this present moment even as this attack fuels reactionary political movements.

Given these sensitivities, we begin this book by taking the opportunity to retrace the beginnings of critical race theory in legal and educational studies, if not earlier. We outline how education scholars pushed critical race theory towards explaining the contextual ways in which different racialised groups experience 'race' and racism in education in the US and beyond. In tracing this genealogy, we engage with the potential limitations of this framework, including both its acceptance of the nation-state as a natural autonomous form, what has been called *methodological*

Color-blind racism is shaped by the liberal belief that individuals, institutions, and nations do and should have equal opportunity to compete in education. According to Eduardo Bonilla-Silva, color-blind racism encompasses four strategies that can mystify how, for example, outcomes produced by educational systems are not the product of racial power:

1. *Abstract liberalism.* Any attempt to redress patterns of racial discrimination through intervening on behalf of a racially subordinate group are seen as 'racist' against the dominant group because it means that people are not being treated equally (rather than equitably).

2. *Naturalisation.* Any uneven racial outcomes in education will be explained as a natural outgrowth of this equal competition, not a historical product of global racial power.

3. *Cultural racism.* Individuals, families, and groups racialized as non-White might, for example, be blamed for not valuing education as much.

4. *Minimisation of racism.* Racism might be acknowledged in shaping racial disparities in education, the role of racism can be dismissed as rather insignificant.

Fig 1.1 The racial ideology of color-blind racism in education (Bonilla-Silva 2022, 82).

nationalism (Wimmer and Glick Schiller 2002), and its unilateral focus on the present moment, what has been called *presentism* (Meghji 2022). These tendencies can interfere with making transnational linkages that help explain how racial domination is both global and deeply historical. For that very reason, we outline how a global critical race perspective in education must be informed by various critical schools of thought, including decolonial studies, post-colonial studies, critical Muslim studies, Black studies, and critical Indigenous studies. These perspectives recognise both the colonial roots of 'race' and racism, as well as the colonial roots of the modern nation-state as a form of racial governance.

While we turn towards these perspectives that challenge 'race' and racism as an intra-national phenomenon, we also recognise that the national orientation within critical race theory of education remains useful. It focuses attention on the dynamic and contextual ways in which 'race' and racism operates through education. The challenge, however, is to not lose sight of the ways in which these local processes draw down from global and deeply historical ideas and practices to protect and preserve White domination on a global scale. We thus focus attention on how this global system of White domination is made and learned through education policy and practice at both national and global levels. We also call attention to the role of knowledge and emotions in education in maintaining and sustaining Whiteness as a global position of power. We then turn to the example of countering violent extremism in education to illustrate the potential application of this global theoretical framework.

This book does not attempt to address the question of 'race' and racism in each educational context throughout the world. This book also does not attempt to compare how national educational contexts from different parts of the world reproduce racialised social systems within their respective contexts. Instead, we have written a more modest book that seeks to provide a theoretical orientation to scholars and students who want to think globally and historically about the nature of 'race' and racism in education. We have opted to publish it in the Palgrave Pivot series for its quicker publication timetable given the urgency of the issues addressed in this book. We also wrote this book for readers within and outside the academy at all levels. However, we are particularly mindful of upper-level undergraduate and graduate students as the audience for this book. We see all our readers as those with the potential to make a theoretical contribution to this body of scholarship through their efforts to explain and combat global racism in education. In this sense, the book is an invitation, if not a provocation, for others to contribute new vocabularies that orient us towards explaining how this global system of White domination is reproduced through education and how it might be contested. To assist with this theoretical development, we have italicised key concepts throughout the book that offer important touchpoints. These italics are meant to help readers identify keywords that they can use to orient themselves in their scholarship and activism. However, at times, these concepts may seem insufficient or simply do not feel quite right in explaining examples that illustrate the interconnectedness of 'race' and racism in education throughout the world. Our readers should employ their own sociological imaginations to develop and contribute concepts when existing concepts do not work in their own analyses. Through these contributions, people will have a better repertoire of conceptual tools to think with as they attempt to refashion educational systems, communities, and practices in ways that might give rise to worlds free from racial domination and elimination.

As we stressed in the opening of this book, there is a need for this global critical race perspective in education now. In our own lives and scholarship, we have struggled with the inadequacy of critical race theory in explaining anti-Muslim racism in education throughout the world. As India, Kashmir, India, Palestine and Western China all show, the stakes are so high. As a result, we hope this book will prove useful for students and scholars seeking to explain the interconnectedness of 'race' and racism across diverse national educational settings. However, this book is not to support explanation for the sake of explanation. Learning to recognise and explain how education maintains and sustains this global system of White domination is necessary, but insufficient. The purpose is to activate a new global imagination. While imagining and making other worlds free from elimination may seem like a daunting task, this global critical race perspective reminds us that the world-system of White domination that we have inherited is a historical product. Making new worlds is therefore possible, and we hope this book contributes in one small way towards that goal—education against elimination.

CHAPTER 2

Critical Race Theory of Education: Beginnings, Limitations, and New Directions

Abstract In Anglo-American culture wars, critical race theory has become a loosely defined and weaponised catchword employed by right-wing political movements to suppress critiques of racism in society. But beyond this bad-faith use of the term, critical race theory has been the most influential theoretical framework since the 1990s for studying how racial injustice is reproduced and contested through education. In this chapter, we trace the beginnings of critical race theory before turning to various good-faith criticisms of this orientation, including its ahistoricism, its methodological nationalism, and its tendency to overlook the necropolitical aspects of global racialized modernity.

Keywords Social theories · Educational Theories · Global Approach · Critical Race Theory · Race · Racism · Decolonization

BEGINNINGS

Edward Saïd once wrote that a beginning, a starting point in any story, not only marks a problem to be studied, but also the position taken by the writer (1975, 13). Establishing any starting point is a choice, and a political one at that. In critical race theory scholarship, the dominant suggestion has been that this school of thought began in American law

© The Author(s) 2026
T. Denmead and A. Shareef, *Rethinking Critical Race Theory*, Palgrave Studies in Race, Inequality and Social Justice in Education,
https://doi.org/10.1007/978-3-032-07749-3_2

schools in the 1960s. Critical race theory emerged as a critical response to the ways in which critical legal studies, a Marxist-informed school of legal thought, had minimised or overlooked the ways in which the law in the US both constructs racial meaning and maintains racial power. However, another point of view might suggest that critical race theory began the moment the American Constitution was drafted and ratified in 1788. In that moment, enslaved people throughout the nation would have learned that this document constructed them as three-fifths of a human, and, in turn, denied them the freedom from tyranny provided to others. As Mari Matsuda (1995) has pointed out, this criticism was most forcefully voiced in the nineteenth century by the abolitionist Frederick Douglass. This critical race theory tradition continued when the Japanese American Citizens League criticised how the US Constitution sanctioned Japanese internment camps in the US during World War II, and when Indigenous people challenged how the US Constitution enshrined the theft of colonial lands across the American Plains and to the Pacific Islands. For Matsuda, these individuals and movements were largely ignored and overlooked by critical legal studies scholars who gained prominence in the US and Europe in the 1960s.

In the 1960s, the critical legal studies movement emerged and challenged the dominant Western legal framework of liberalism from a Marxist perspective. This liberal view frames the law as an independent and autonomous system, one that is separate from and above society. From this perspective, the legal system rules impartially on whether laws have been broken. This 'rule of law' is a fundamental value of liberal societies. However, activists in the 1960s began to question the presumed autonomy of the law in liberal and capitalistic societies through their reading of Marxism. Rather than seeing the law as objective, neutral and impartial, their Marxist approach framed the law as an *ideological state apparatus* (Althusser 1977). From this standpoint, legal systems in capitalist societies construct meaning through various mechanisms—from writing law to rendering court rulings—in ways that legitimise the accumulation of capital through the exploitation of workers.

Other US intellectuals and activists shared this Marxist suspicion of Western legal systems as objective and neutral. However, they were wary of an approach that avoided a close consideration of 'race'. Indeed, the dominant Marxist tendency at that time was to approach racism merely as an ideological byproduct of capitalism rather than an endemic feature of Western societies. From the Marxist point of view, class is the real force and factor in shaping unequal societies; racism just works in service of maintaining class hegemony. This group of critical race legal scholars began to challenge this classical Marxist perspective. These scholars were mainly people of colour, often African-American, who had witnessed and participated in the American struggle for civil rights. This American Civil Rights Movement challenged how the nation's political and legal system had sanctioned and legitimised racial segregation, exclusion, and violence throughout the country's history. As a result, these scholars were primarily concerned with how 'race' and racism in the US was established and elaborated through its liberal system of political and economic governance. These scholars developed the framework now known as critical race theory.

In the 1970s, critical race theory scholars in legal studies started to advance several ideas that are now considered foundational to this framework. First, they argued that 'race' has no biological basis. (This recognition is denoted in this book using quotation marks: 'race'). As much as thinkers and scientists have tried over hundreds of years, no one has ever found any physical substance, either macroscopic or microscopic, that can be used to classify, sort, and rank people within different human categories. Alternatively, critical race scholars have argued that the American legal system constructs 'race' and ascribes meaning to different racial categories. This construction of racial categories depends upon assigning meanings to them based on their imagined relative superiority and inferiority, their imagined relative value and valuelessness. For example, the American legal system has historically constructed American people with African ancestry as Black and then ruled in ways that established and repeated various pejorative and life-threatening meanings assigned to Blackness (see Fig. 2.1). As we will see, because racial categories have no basis in material reality, they are highly elastic and expansive. Racial categories slip and slide as they do different kinds of work in producing relations of racial power across various contexts. While highly variable, this racial construction and ascription of meaning based on 'race' is a process now commonly referred to as *racialisation* (see Hochman 2019).[1] The American legal system thus established Whiteness

---

[1] This process of *racialisation* is different from, but related to, the process captured by the term *othering*. Othering refers to the ways in which divisions are constructed between 'us' and 'them' in ways that construct 'them' as both foreign and a threat. Racialisation more explicitly refers to the ways in which people are imagined to be fundamentally

as the natural and legitimate 'race' of American citizens and Blackness, and other racialised categories, as subordinate races that must be subjected to racial power in order to advance the nation's interests.

While early critical race theory scholars argued that 'race' itself is not real, they insisted 'race' has real material effects on the distribution of resources, power, and opportunity (K. Crenshaw et al. 1995, xxix). The

A brief history outlines how the American legal system constructed meaning about 'race' and sanctioned the uneven distribution of social, political, legal, and economic rights and opportunities based on those ascribed meanings. The founding document outlining the system of governance in the United States constructed enslaved people as less than human. This constitution stipulated that enslaved people would count as three-fifths of one citizen for the purposes of determining taxation and representation in government. They were, of course, not entitled to any rights. This compromise gave Southern states disproportionate representation in the United States Congress. Subsequent US Supreme Court rulings determined that enslaved people were incapable of bearing rights and responsibilities in this liberal democracy. In the *Dred Scott v. Sandford* (1857), Dred Scott and his wife were enslaved people who sued for their freedom and the freedom of their daughters. The Supreme Court ruled that they did not have any legal standing to bring this case forward because no one with African ancestry could be a citizen in the US. This legal system also constructed meaning that suggested Black people should and must be treated as a contagion or threat. In the *Plessy v. Ferguson* case (1896) before the US Supreme Court, Homer Plessy, a person of mixed-race heritage, sued against the charge that he had violated a Louisiana state law by sitting in a 'Whites-only' train car. Plessy and his lawyers claimed the state law was unconstitutional. The US Supreme Court ruled against him, thus sanctioning the 'Jim Crow' laws throughout the South that legalised and enforced racial segregation. The ruling claimed that segregation still allowed for equal treatment ('separate but equal'). This ruling was not overturned until the famous *Brown v. Board of Education* (1954) that ruled that segregated education systems were unequal.

Fig. 2.1 A history of Supreme Court rulings that demonstrate how the American legal system has constructed Blackness and protected the interests of Whiteness.

different kinds of human and then ranked accordingly based on their perceived relative value and superiority. Othering often depends on racialisation to construct 'them' as not only foreign, but a different type of human with a different degree of value.

construction of racial categories and meanings necessarily leads to patterns of racial domination in society.
that are sustained and maintained over time. These patterns unevenly distribute a variety of advantages and disadvantages, from economic to cultural ones, across racial categories. From this perspective, 'race' and racism must always be considered together; they are inseparable. Moreover, critical race theory perspective does not approach racism as the overt actions of prejudiced individuals against people they deem to be different and inferior. Instead, racism is approached in a structural and material way rather than an individualistic one. This structural approach indicates that there is an uneven pattern of relationships between groups of people based on the distribution of meanings associated with each of those groups (Bonilla-Silva 1997, 469, see footnote 5). This *material* approach indicates that there is a distribution of various properties—personhood, citizenship, income, wealth, and land—for those who participate in those social and structural arrangements (Bonilla-Silva 1997, 469 see footnote 5).[2] A critical race theory approach to structure and materiality therefore recognises that these patterns and this distribution are unevenly shaped and preserved through racial power.

Early critical race theory scholars also challenged framings of Whiteness as a hereditary substance or trait that is passed from one generation to the next. Instead, they framed Whiteness as a relational position within an always-contested racial ordering of society. In other words, Whiteness only exists through a relation with other 'races' placed in a racial hierarchy. For example, Whiteness occupies a superior and dominant position and Blackness within a matrix of power through a relation with Blackness that is deemed to be inferior and subordinate. This dominant position for Whiteness yields social, cultural, political, and economic power over other racial groups within this hierarchy. Moreover, Whiteness signifies various meanings such as beauty, intelligence, morality, advancement, and accumulation. Those who are given the status of being White therefore benefit from this hierarchy and cultural significations. For this reason, Cheryl

---

[2] *Materiality* is a Marxist concept that refers to the loss of humanity that arises through capitalism based on workers' producing material objects that no longer belong to them and through consumers measuring their life's value based on how many material commodities they accumulate (see Miller 2018). A structural account of racism builds on this tradition through recognising how racist social systems measure the value of life based on greater or lesser proximity to Whiteness, and distribute various material objects (land, wealth, commodities) according to those measurements.

Harris, an influential critical race theory scholar, argued that Whiteness should be understood as a form of *property* (Harris 1993). From this perspective, the status that comes with being identified as White is a 'valuable asset—one that people, irrespective of their 'race', can seek to protect and pass on to their kin' (Harris 1993, 277). Harris (1993) argued that American law has historically affirmed, legitimated, and protected this 'treasured property' through, for example, sanctioning racial segregation (277). This framing of Whiteness as a form of property has influenced Black studies scholars such as George Lipsitz. He argued that people, no matter whether they are White or not, can 'invest' in the value of Whiteness through expending time and energy in establishing and reestablishing this position of racial dominance (2006, viii). Lipsitz referred to this phenomenon as the *possessive investment in Whiteness* (Lipsitz 2006).

Early critical race theory scholars also argued that racism, and the protection of Whiteness as a treasured asset, are endemic to US liberal democracy (Bell 2018). From this perspective, the legal system within US liberal democracy has always, and will always continue to, reproduce existing patterns of racial domination that protect Whiteness. The American legal system has only historically extended liberal democratic rights, economic opportunity, and political power to racially subordinated groups if doing so further protected or enhanced the value of Whiteness. Indeed, Derrick Bell (1980) argued that one of the primary drivers for the passage of civil rights legislation in the 1960s was the fact that American practices of racial segregation and exclusion compromised its global position in the Cold War. It extended those freedoms to protect the nation's global hegemony, to protect both its political and economic interests. Bell (1980) referred to this principle as *interest convergence* (523). This principle means that racially inferiorised people in the US will only achieve racial equality when it converges with the interests of White people (Bell 1980, 523).

Given the endemic nature of racism in American liberal democracy, the challenge from a critical race theory perspective is therefore not to reform this legal system. Rather, the challenge, no matter how daunting, requires reimagining the very constitutional fabric of the nation. This reimagining requires centring the perspectives of those who have endured the effects of this legal system from a racially subjugated position, even if they have not been understood as legal scholars per se. Mari Matsuda referred to this method as 'looking to the bottom' (Matsuda 1995, 63). This methodological approach illustrates the influence of W.E.B Du Bois's

(2008) concept of *double consciousness* on critical race theory. Double consciousness holds that those subjected beneath the colour line have a powerful insight into the workings of racial power because they can both see their own humanity and see how their humanity is denied by those who perceive them as inferior and valueless (Du Bois 2008, 8). Building on this concept, critical race theory foregrounds those who have this special capability of seeing racial power from both dominant and subordinate positions, a principle that has informed its methodological preference for *counter-storytelling* (Solórzano and Yosso 2002). Through counter-storytelling, those who experience racial subordination destabilise the apparent naturalness and legitimacy of racial power through calling to account dominant racial ideologies and their effects on their own lives.

Early critical race theory legal scholars have also examined how relations of power operate at the intersection of various aspects of social identity. Drawing on the Black feminist tradition, Kimberlé Crenshaw coined the term *intersectionality* to argue that 'the intersection of racism and sexism factors into Black women's lives in ways that cannot be captured wholly by looking at the race or gender dimensions of those experiences separately' (1991, 1244). Contributing to this line of thought and activism, Patricia Hill Collins distinguished this concept of intersectionality from the *matrix of domination* (2009, 21). The matrix of domination refers to how power operates through intersections of, say, race, class, and gender. In recent years, there has been a significant debate over how intersectionality is now often used in ways that do not foreground the intersectional oppression of Black women (see Nash 2019). Nonetheless, intersectionality has been highly influential in establishing how various systems, including the legal one, do not produce relations of power through only one dimension of human experience, such as 'race'. As such, critical race theory seeks to account for the matrix of domination rather than merely the spectrum of racial domination between Blackness and Whiteness.

In the 1990s, critical race theory in legal studies began to have a significant impact on US education scholarship. Scholars began to interrogate how educational systems and practices are implicated in maintaining and sustaining racism in US society (Ladson-Billings and Tate IV 1995). Echoing the key principles in legal studies outlined above, Daniel Solórzano (1997) then identified the following five *tenets* of critical race theory of education:

1. *The centrality and intersectionality of race and racism.* Racism is a permanent feature of US society and racism intersects with other forms of subordination that arise through gender, class, sexuality, language, disability, culture, and immigrant status;
2. *The challenge to dominant liberal ideology.* Liberalism sustains racism and protects White interests through claims to objectivity, impartiality, meritocracy, and equal opportunity in educational institutions;
3. *The commitment to social justice.* The aim is not merely explanation, but rather the production of an equitable society in which everyone, no matter their background, has the equal opportunity to flourish.
4. *The centrality of experiential knowledge.* The embodied and experiential knowledge of people who experience racisms should be foregrounded through methods including storytelling, parables, biographies, and so forth; and,
5. *The interdisciplinary perspective.* A mono-disciplinary and ahistorical analysis of racial power is limited given the nature of how racial power operates in multiple spheres of life (6–7).

Through these tenets, critical race theory in education emerged as a radical alternative to the dominant educational approach to engaging with difference and diversity in the US at that time—*multiculturalism.* The aim of multicultural education is to cultivate citizens who respect and value human diversity. In their seminal paper calling for critical race theory in education, Gloria Ladson-Billings and William Tate criticised multicultural education for teaching knowledge in service of racial domination (Ladson-Billings and Tate IV 1995, 62). For example, well-meaning teachers might try to teach their students an appreciation for human diversity through introducing 'trivial examples and artifacts of cultures such as eating ethnic or cultural foods, singing songs or dancing, reading folktales' (Ladson-Billings and Tate IV 1995, 61). This approach can reinforce the *essentialist* belief that different racially inferiorised groups are bound by an essence that is fundamentally primitive, backwards, and monocultural. As a result, multicultural education from an uncritical perspective, or one that does not address questions of power and knowledge, can maintain and sustain a society structured in racial dominance rather than transform it.

Early education scholars of critical race theory also challenged a dominant approach to knowledge production—that of *logical positivism*. Logical positivism rejects any statements that cannot be verifiably observed, measured, and proven. From this perspective, any claim of racism in education requires verifiable proof that racism did in fact cause a particular outcome. This approach is often used to dismiss claims that racism has in fact played a role in shaping educational institutions and experiences. In other words, without indubitable evidence that establishes causality, accusations of racism can be called into question, if not denied. Logical positivism holds that prejudicial beliefs, intentions, and actions must be observed, measured, and proven to verify whether racism did in fact happen. Not only is that difficult to prove, but this focus on individuals and their intentions also distracts from the structural nature of racism whereby various advantages and disadvantages are distributed across a social pattern over time without people necessarily or willingly having racist ideas or willingly acting in overtly racist ways. As a result, critical race theory of education shifted attention away from trying to prove that racism exists in education or that individual actors are responsible for racism in educational contests. Instead, critical race theory focuses attention on explaining how education is a key force in sustaining a social system that produces racist outcomes.

DEVELOPMENTS

Since its beginnings in educational studies, critical race theory has evolved to engage with more diverse manifestations of 'race' and racism in schools and other contexts. This evolution has been shaped most significantly by Black feminist concepts of intersectionality and the matrix of domination. Critical race theory has thus produced what have been referred to variously as 'spin-off movements' (Delgado and Stefancic 2023, 7), 'offshoots' (Gaztambide-Fernández, Kraehe, and Carpenter II 2018, 5), or 'micro-theoretical perspectives' (Misawa 2012, 242). Education and legal scholars and activists have developed these offshoots to account for the ways in which racial power operates in contextually specific and intersectional ways for different groups. Examples include: QueerCrit (Misawa 2012); Tribal Crit (Brayboy 2005); LatCrit (Solórzano and Yosso 2001); Asian Crit (Iftikar and Museus 2018); DesiCrit (Harpalani 2013); DisCrit (Annamma et al. 2013); MusCrit (Ali 2022); and critical Whiteness studies (Matias et al. 2014). Each of these offshoots takes the central tenets or principles of critical race theory outlined in the previous section and then modifies and applies them to the experiences and realities of groups in question. By adopting these tenets for each contextual consideration, these offshoots are oriented towards producing critical forms of knowledge that counter the specificities of subjugation within a matrix of domination.

MusCrit provides a useful illustration of one such offshoot. Noor Ali (2022) developed MusCrit after recognising that the 'Muslim experience does not find representation in CRT' and doing so is necessary to 'acknowledge the racialisation of Muslims regardless of their 'race" (348), regardless of whether or not, for example, they are in colour-based terms Black, Brown, or White. It is important to add that people can also be racialised as Muslim regardless of their religion. She developed MusCrit to account for how people racialised as Muslim are constructed in racial terms, placed in a racial hierarchy, and in turn, experience racism in distinctive ways. From this point of view, Muslim people, as well as people who are mistaken as Muslim, experience racialisation and racism through both religion and other identity markers including skin colour, facial hair, clothing, language, names, ethnicity, and nationality (Selod and Embrick 2013). Through the 'Global War on Terror'—an American-led international counter-terrorism and counterinsurgency campaign—Arab, African, and South Asian Muslims have been racialised as individuals who are barbaric and incompatible with Western civilisation (Daulatzai and Rana 2018; Rana 2011). In addition, people who are not Muslim have been positioned as Muslim through a variety of ways, including the misreading of people's religious signifiers. This experience of racialisation and racism affects people who are both Muslim and positioned as Muslims in educational contexts (Sirin and Fine 2008). For example, young Muslim women in Britain experience constant suspicion in public contexts, including schools. Amina Shareef (2023), an author of this book, has argued that this constant suspicion and threat of physical violence produces a kind of lived experience that she terms 'a besieged life' (21). Similarly, Nicole Nguyen (2019) has shown how young Muslim people in American schools are positioned as 'incipient terrorists' through counter extremism policies and practices (1). Across these two contexts, this constant suspicion causes young Muslim people, and people who fear being mistaken as Muslim, to alter their everyday behaviour, including their religious and clothing practices. They do so to protect themselves from overt racism, direct physical violence, or being reported to state security apparatuses.

Noor Ali (2022) thus developed MusCrit in order to provide 'relevance and validation' within critical race theory to these educational experiences of young Muslim people (348). As an offshoot, MusCrit challenges the dominant tendency in educational studies to frame Muslim people as those who experience stereotyping, othering, and xenophobia, but not racialisation and racism. This dominant tendency is rooted in the assumption that Muslim people do not experience racialisation and racism because Islam is a religion, not a 'race'. However, 'race' can be applied to different social groups that are typically not thought of as racial precisely because 'race' has no material basis. 'Race' is what has been called a *floating signifier* (Hall and Media Education Foundation 1996). This view reflects the *anti-essentialist* perspective to 'race' that is key to critical race theory. 'Race' is not considered to have any essence or core characteristic that defines it. Grounded in these assumptions, Noor Ali's offshoot forces the recognition of how racism structurally subordinates Muslim people, and people who are not Muslim but racialised as Muslim, in education through intersections of culture, phenotype, skin colour, gender, and other attributes. MusCrit thus calls for counter-narratives that allow young people in education to name their experiences and realities of anti-Muslim racism in education. This example shows how scholars can and should carve out a 'niche' in critical race theory, as Noor Ali (2022, 348) puts it, to challenge different manifestations of structural racism, in this case, anti-Muslim racism.

This turn towards more intersectional approaches to critical race theory in educational studies has been significant. There is always the risk that critical race theory focuses exclusively on the White-Black racial binary. In this reductive approach, racial contestation in education is only framed as a struggle between two groups, Black and White people. Of course, this racial dualism is important to acknowledge. In a White dominant world, these two poles—Black and White—are fundamental in structuring relative positions of racial power. However, this binary can also distract from and disregard the nuanced experiences of other groups racialised as 'non-White'. It can also lead to thinking that seeks to compare which group is the 'most oppressed' within a racial system of power rather than seeing different manifestations of 'race' and racism as interdependent and intersecting within a global system of racial and power. As a result, this second generation has been necessary to the development of critical race theory in educational studies. However, these offshoots have largely not addressed the pressing ways in which educational systems and practices are implicated in reproducing not only a racial order at the national level, but also a global system of White domination. In this way, we are less concerned with establishing a new niche within critical race theory. Instead, we are more interested in providing an orientation to critical race theory that accounts for the long and global history of 'race' and racism in education.

Some scholars have begun to point towards this transnational orientation to critical race theory. For example, Stephen Nelson (2020) points out that critical race theory of education might return to innovation in legal studies to address this important need. He argues that 'Third World Approaches to International Law' provides a useful framework for doing this theoretical work, as well as the work of political resistance (Nelson 2020, 307). This approach links current international law to the colonial project that commenced at or around the sixteenth century as the transatlantic slave trade' (Nelson 2020, 308). While we welcome this call for a more transnational orientation to critical race theory, Nelson maintains both a focus on the American context, as well as the White-Black racial binary. His principal concern is, after all, how 'White Americans have failed to acknowledge how education policies in the United States and the rejection of. Human rights treaties serve to subject Black Americans to Third World treatment', which is then 'similar to the very Third World treatments that othered peoples in international contexts suffer' (Nelson 2020, 330, 331). There is scope for developing an approach to critical race theory that recognises the global nature of anti-Black racism and American parochialism that has shaped so much of critical race theory scholarship. With that in mind, we turn to discuss three key limitations of critical race theory scholarship in educational studies.

LIMITATIONS

There is an obvious risk in discussing the limitations of critical race theory in this moment in which we write. After all, 'critical race theory' has been weaponised in recent years to protect Whiteness as a treasured property asset. Nonetheless, scholars and students must continue to engage with good-faith debates about critical race theory. Engaging with these debates, and well-intentioned criticisms, does not mean that scholars and students should respond to forced political debates about the strength of critical race theory from leftist or conservative points of view. Instead, engaging with these debates means comparing the strengths and weaknesses of critical race theory as a social explanation in relation to other competing perspectives, such as liberalism, Marxism, post-colonial theory, and decolonial thought. In recent years, sociological perspectives and decolonial thought have offered different points of view on 'race' and racism that illustrate three limitations of critical race theory of education. It is important to acknowledge these criticisms to continue to develop this perspective in ways that respond to the examples that we are witnessing, including genocide.

The first criticism is the tendency within critical race theory to only describe and interpret racism in educational contexts rather than explain how educational systems and practices reproduce uneven racial patterns over time. From this point of view, critical race theory has provided a set of methodological tools, such as counter-storytelling, to counter dominant racial ideologies. It has also provided normative commitments, or beliefs in how social phenomena should be approached. Critical race theory, for example, allows scholars to recognise that 'race' and racism shapes educational contexts without having to prove it in some quantified way. But providing methodological tools and normative commitments does not make critical race theory a *social theory*. Ali Meghji (2021), a sociologist of 'race' and racism, argues that educational studies using this critical race perspective are often cut short by not developing a set of concepts that can be used to 'understand the production and reproduction of racism *outside of the empirical confines of the original studies*' (350, author's emphasis). Meghji (2021) therefore challenges scholars working in education to approach critical race theory as a social theory, such as Marxism, rather than an assemblage of methodologies and commitments. As a social theory, critical race theory must search for concepts that explain how education contributes to sustaining and maintaining—or *reproducing*—systems structured in racial dominance. Reproduction is a sociological term that refers to how asymmetrical social patterns—patterns that are produced and sustained through the uneven and contested distribution of power—persist over time. As a social theory, critical race theory must therefore seek to explain how educational systems and practices contribute to the reproduction of broader entrenched racial patterns.

The second criticism of critical race theory is its tendency to approach educational systems and the racialised societies in which they are embedded only at a local and national scale. As we have noted, critical race theory was developed first in the American context before being translated and extended to other contexts, including, for example, Britain, India, Australia, and Spain (e.g. Warmington 2020; Goodnight 2017). As a result, this approach can be called into question for its relevance in explaining other national contexts that do not share the same legal history and educational system as the US. Critical race theory can also be called into question for its relevance in national contexts that do not feature the same racial differences and antagonisms. As American scholars studying and teaching in Britain, we hear these criticisms all the time. Our concern, however, is not so much with the problem of translating or extending critical race theory from the US context to educational contexts in other parts of the world. Our assumption is that 'race' and racism is global in nature. For this reason, sociologists in recent years have been developing global critical 'race' and racism perspectives (Meghji 2022; Christian 2019; Weiner 2012). We join these efforts while recognising that a global approach to a critical race theory has been somewhat absent from educational studies until recently. This transnational approach to critical race theory has been driven by the attention on international Chinese students experiencing racism in the American higher education system (Yu et al. 2024; Kim 2022; Yao et al. 2019), as well as through recognising the global nature of anti-Black racism (Busey and Coleman-King 2023). This trend points to the recognition of the need to explain how interconnected educational systems and practices across the world reproduce a global system rooted in White domination.

Curiously, traces of this global orientation to a critical race theory can be found in its early educational scholarship. Indeed, Christopher Busey and Chonika Coleman-King (2023) write that so much of critical race theory scholarship in education overlooks 'the global intellectual heritage of critical Black social and political thought constitutive' of this perspective (1333). After all, W.E.B. Du Bois (1940) was a global race scholar who theorised the role of the colour line in production of what he called *The White World*. At the end of Gloria Ladson-Billings and William Tate's (1995) seminal paper 'Towards a critical race theory of education', they pointed to this global orientation to 'race' and racism informed by critical Black social and political thought. At the end of the paper, they quote Marcus Garvey, an early twentieth-century Jamaican political activist who was a proponent of racial separatism and Black global solidarity. 'In a world of wolves one should go armed', Garvey wrote (and they quote). 'And one of the most powerful defensive weapons within the reach of Negroes is the practice of race first in all parts of the world' (quoted in Ladson-Billings and Tate IV 1995, 62). The phrasing at the end of the passage—'race first in all parts of the world'—points towards this global orientation to 'race' and racism rooted in Black thought. Garvey saw 'race' and racism, and anti-Black racism in particular, as forces that shape all parts of the world in an interconnected way. However, this global orientation has remained significantly underdeveloped by education scholars who employ critical race theory, perhaps a reflection of American parochialism in critical scholarship (see Dabashi 2019). Indeed, both of us are Americans who live and study in Britain. It was only until we moved from the US and began studying 'race' and racism in education with respect to the international figure of the Muslim political subject that we saw the need for a more globally oriented approach.

A third criticism of critical race theory is its tendency to focus on the present without much consideration of the past (see Meghji 2022). Education scholars who employ critical race theory tend to focus on contemporary educational contexts and practices. This orientation towards the present has been influenced by the influence of legal thought on critical race theory in educational studies. For example, Kimberlé Crenshaw (2011) once defined critical race theory in legal studies as a framework that attends to 'the ways that racial power is understood and articulated in the post-civil rights era' (1261). This focus on racial power after the civil rights era means that critical race theory focuses on the period after the 1960s, but not before it. There is a good reason for this contemporary focus. Critical race theory scholars always seek to challenge the view that racism in the US context is merely an odious stench left over from transatlantic slavery that will, over time, dissipate through social progress (and education!). As a result, education scholars who employ critical race theory have been ambivalent about focusing on racism in the past to make clear that contemporary racism does not manifest in the same ways as it did in the past. As a result, the tendency has been to focus on how the evolving meanings of racial categories, or *racial formations,* and the changing nature of racism, maintain and sustain a historical racial structure (Omi and Winant 1994).

This focus on the present, however, has one important limitation. The global system of White domination has a long history. Indeed, its history predates the founding of not only the US, but also the nation-state as a political form. While there have been numerous debates about when the Western global history of 'race' and racism began, the dominant view is that this history began in the long sixteenth century with the emergence of the modern world, or *modernity* (see Hall et al. 2011). Given this starting point, and perhaps even earlier, it is necessary to take a long historical view of White domination. Without doing so, it can be difficult to make transnational linkages to understand this global system, and to understand how local and national education systems and practices interact with it. At the same time, an eye to this long history does not require an abandonment of the contextually specific and dynamic ways in which 'race' and racism operates at local and national levels. Indeed, this focus on the local and national context should be preserved as this global orientation points us towards the historical interconnectedness of those contexts.

CHAPTER 3

Towards a Global Critical Race Theory of Education

Abstract The dominant tendency within critical race theory of education has been to focus on how educational systems and practices reproduce racialized social systems within local and national contexts. It has privileged the knowledge produced by racialised groups through story-telling to counter dominant racial ideologies. Given that racial knowledge and emotions circulate globally, the challenge today for educational scholars, students, and activists is to explain how local and national educational systems draw from global forms of racism to maintain racialised social systems within nations *and* across the world. Drawing on insights from decolonial thought, critical Muslim studies, and Black thought, we outline a global critical race theory approach to educational scholarship and practice.

Keywords Social theories · Educational Theories · Global Approach · Critical Race Theory · Race · Racism · Decolonization

Critical race theory was forged through a deep suspicion of the US as a liberal nation-state. For example, Derrick Bell (2018) argued that the US would protect White interests at the expense of people of colour, and particularly, Black people, in perpetuity. Liberalism as an economic and political philosophy is principally concerned with maximising individual

© The Author(s) 2026
T. Denmead and A. Shareef, *Rethinking Critical Race Theory*, Palgrave Studies in Race, Inequality and Social Justice in Education,
https://doi.org/10.1007/978-3-032-07749-3_3

freedom and the accumulation of property. However, in the US, from the nation's inception, freedom and property were encoded in the law as exclusive possessions of White people. When the legal sanctioning of racial discrimination was eliminated in the 1960s, liberal values such as equality and meritocracy provided the basis for protecting those historical advantages moving forward. Through this orientation to the US as a liberal nation-state, critical race theory has since been translated to other national contexts but still has the tendency to frame racial inequalities and injustices as a national phenomenon rather than a global one. The interconnected nature of 'race' and racism across the globe points to the need for this global critical race perspective.

Every theoretical orientation must, at least implicitly, begin with a theory of the world. Our perspective begins with the recognition that we inhabit a global system of racial power that requires individuals, groups, institutions, and nation-states to move away from racialised and colonial positions that are deemed to be racially inferior and historically immature. This demand to become more proximate to Whiteness and Europeanness is not only an attempt to accrue its material and symbolic benefits, but also to avoid exposure to state regulation, state violence, and state-induced death (Christian 2019). Nation-states throughout the world can become more proximate to Whiteness and Europeanness within this global system of racial and colonial domination through the regulation, expulsion, and killing of those who signify the lack of what are thought to be the exclusive properties of Whiteness and Europeanness—rationality, intelligence, beauty, wealth, and advancement. This global arrangement signifies the continual failure of the modern world to live up to the European promise of universal sovereignty, progress, equality, freedom, and tolerance. Indeed, the singular path of development available to nation-states in the modern world has been, and continues to be, one that demands the regulation, expulsion, and death of racialised and colonised populations. These populations are posited in historically and contextually specific ways as threats to the purity and the advancement of this global system of White domination when they refuse attempts to become more proximate to Whiteness and Europeanness.

Educationists must pay attention to the ways in which education systems, institutions, and practices throughout the world are implicated in the reproduction of this global racial order. Educational systems are a universal feature of the modern world. Indeed, these systems are a key pillar in the formation and continuity of any given nation-state. Critical race theory must therefore recognise that not all nation-states are liberal states, and non-liberal nation-states are implicated in maintaining and sustaining a global system based on White dominance. This perspective must also recognise that the nation-state as a political form was a European invention that was formed in Europe through imperial and colonial projects abroad and then was exported abroad through its imperial and colonial projects. From this perspective, the nation-state is fundamentally a racial and colonial apparatus forged through the history of modernity (Dragoş 2024). The nation-state is a racial apparatus because it is predicated on establishing and maintaining the purity of its population—imagined as 'the people' in nativist and populist terms—through the regulation, expulsion, and death of populations deemed to be foreign, inferior, valueless, and threatening (Goldberg 2002). The nation-state is a colonial apparatus because the historical maturity of nations, or their degree of relative development and advancement, is measured against arbitrary norms, beliefs, values, and standards that are associated with Western nations (e.g. GDP, secularisation, Whiteness of the population, etc.) (See Chapter 4 in Kennedy 2016).

Given these endemic racial and colonial features of this political form, nation-states, as well as individuals and groups within them, gain relative power within this global system by their proximity to Whiteness as a dominant position (Christian 2019). Education is one of the ways in which this process unfolds. It is through education that Whiteness and it is through education that racial and colonial difference is regulated, if not eliminated (Sriprakash et al. 2022). As a result, a more global critical race orientation to education must recognise that educational systems are not merely reproduced in the reproduction of racialised social systems at the local and national level. They are implicated in the reproduction of a global system that has a long and continuous history. This assumption is necessary to recognise that the challenge before us is not merely imagining an alternative to, say, a liberal nation-state, but rather imagining alternative global configurations to the one we inhabit, one that is now centuries, if not a millenium, in the making.

History

One of the exceptions to the presentism of critical race theory in educational studies has been Tribal Crit. Tribal Crit recognises that an analysis of the present must recognise a long and continuous history of 'the lives and experiences of tribal peoples since contact with Europeans over 500 years ago' (Brayboy 2005, 430). This long historical orientation found in Tribal Crit is more typical within other critical schools of thought including critical Indigenous studies, Black studies, post-colonial studies, decolonial studies, and critical Muslim studies. These critical traditions approach the history of 'race' and racism as an endemic feature of the modern world. From this vantage point, the history of 'race' and racism predates the emergence of not only the United States, but also the nation-state as a political form that emerged through modernity. Critical race theory can therefore learn from these perspectives in taking a long histor-ical approach to 'race' and racism, one that recognises the transnational continuity of 'race' and racism throughout the history of modernity. Modernity is a slippery concept to define, and there has been considerable debate about when the history of modernity begins. That said, there is no singular or verifiable time or space when modernity emerged, and estab-lishing possible starting points and locations is not just about examining archival records. Choosing possible starting points for modernity requires paying attention to how choosing one time and location over another inevitably produces blind spots that limit our ability to understand both historical and contemporary phenomena of 'race' and racism. In this way, choosing any starting point reflects vested interests in political struggles over modernity itself (Said 1975).

Modernity is generally understood as a moment in history in which Western European and Christian people began to see themselves as capable of shaping the history of the world for the betterment of humanity. The beginning of modernity marks a moment in which Western European Christian and White people began to see themselves as capable of emancipating the world from the immaturity, intolerance, irrationality, and superstition that plagued the era that preceded it. In Western educational systems, the history of modernity is often taught as an intra-European phenomenon; its key historical events include, for example, the Enlightenment and the French Revolution in the seventeenth and eigh-teenth centuries. For decades, however, various critical perspectives have pointed out that the history of modernity was not an intra-European phenomenon, but rather a global one (Dussel 2000). Moreover, scholars have pointed out that key moments in history, such as the Haitian Revo-lution, reveal that it was not only Europeans who could attempt to emancipate the world from its darkness (James 2001).

Nonetheless, modernity marks a historical moment in which Western Christian White Europeans began to imagine themselves as superior and more historically advanced through their encounters with populations they deemed to be fundamentally inferior and primitive both within and outside the European continent. Through these global encounters, the Latin American decolonial scholar Enrique Dussel (2000) argues, 'the whole planet became the space of one world history' (470). In this moment, or series of moments, Western Christian White Europeans nominated themselves as the stewards of the planet and the exclusive signifier of humanity itself. They imagined themselves as the standard bearer for global humanity, an imaginary that could only have been possible through establishing relations of dominance over different populations throughout the world based on their culture and their colour. This relation established 'race' as the conceptual framework for differentiating and hierarchising human life, and racialisation became the contextually specific process for making 'race'. This establishment of racial superiority meant that Western Christian White Europeans saw themselves as holding a moral obligation to develop subordinate racialised populations that were not yet ready for bearing the responsibility of shaping world history. In this way, these populations were not only constructed in racial terms as inferior, subordinate, and valueless. They were also constructed in colonial terms as if they were historically immature, with their distance from the centre of the world operating as a proxy for their relative advancement. They were thus positioned in need of development through various colonial projects, including education itself. When this racial and colonial ordering of the world was met with resistance, Western Christian White Europeans justified brutal violence on the basis that they had the rightful duty to emancipate the world from darkness (Dussel 2000).

This decolonial perspective on the history of the modern world challenges conventional histories of 'race' and racism. Of course, there is a dominant tendency to believe that 'race' and racism began and died with the rise and ostensible fall of biological race science in the eighteenth and nineteenth centuries. This perspective is wrong because 'race' as a biological concept is not the only way, or even the dominant way, that human difference and inferiority/superiority have been constructed throughout the history of the modern world. In this long history, culture has been the dominant way in which 'race' has been understood. As such, we challenge conventional views, shaped by anthropology as a modern disciplinary formation, that see 'ethnicity' (or culture) as a separate concept from 'race'.[1] From our perspective, populations that are subordinated and inferiorised through culture are populations that are racialised. This cultural process of racialisation has a long history, one that began through encounters with religious difference (Grosfoguel 2016). This longer history must be recognised to understand how the contemporary global system of White domination is predicated on the racial subjection of various groups–including religious ones–in distinctive, yet similar, ways today.

Decolonial thought has been particularly influential in recent educational studies (see, for example, Dussel 2000; Wynter 1995). The 'decolonial turn' has multiple beginnings across different locations and contexts, each bound by 'making colonialism a fundamental problem, and of conceiving of decoloniality as an unfinished project' (Maldonado-Torres 2017, 124). The concept of 'decolonizing' has been used in education in a variety of ways (see Shahjahan et al. 2022), thus making it susceptible to criticism for its ambiguity and even for its incorporation into projects that are at odds with its critique of the modern world. For example, scholars have noted how the Hindu supremacist movement in India, or Hindutva, has co-opted the vocabulary of decolonise to assert that turning to Hindu supremacist ideas and concepts is a way of indigenising knowledge production that was threatened by British colonialism (Kliemann 2023). However, this ideology of Hindu supremacism maintains both the caste system and the threat to Muslim communities within India and occupied Kashmir. Drawing on decolonial thought therefore requires some careful consideration and some caution.

Nonetheless, we have been particularly influenced by decolonial perspectives from a Latin American and Caribbean perspective. These perspectives have not only challenged the Eurocentric view that modernity began with the intra-European phenomenon of the Enlightenment.

---

[1] 'Race' is often constructed as different from ethnicity. From this vantage point, 'race' is imagined to be the product of biological difference whereas ethnicity is imagined to be the product of cultural difference (e.g. heritage, language, religion). This division between 'race' as a biological substance and 'ethnicity' as cultural difference is highly problematic. In fact, it is the historical product of modern disciplinary formations in the eighteenth and nineteenth centuries that were organised around particular bodies of knowledge and intellectual concerns. The notion of ethnic or cultural difference is the historical product of anthropological thought whereas the notion of 'race' as a material substance is the historical product of biological thought (or 'race science'). Once we recognise that 'race' cannot be reduced to a material or biological substance—skin colour, blood, genes—then this distinction between 'race' and ethnicity becomes harder to maintain.

They also challenged post-colonial perspectives that critiqued this Euro-centrism. For example, Edward Saïd (1978) argued that a significant moment marking the beginning of Western modernity was not the French Revolution, but rather, Napoleon's invasion of Egypt in 1798. For him, this invasion marked a moment in which the West began to conceive itself as responsible for developing a more primitive and barbaric East to advance humanity. While Saïd's decentring of the Eurocentric view of modernity was welcomed by decolonial scholars, this history of modernity was neither considered long enough nor reflective of the complexity of racialised and Orientalist encounters within and across continents. For these scholars, the year 1492 is significant because, as we will see, it is the year that the last Muslim state on the European continent was defeated, and it was also the year Christopher Columbus crossed the Atlantic Ocean and encountered Indigenous people in the Americas. However, choosing the year 1492 as the starting point of Western modernity can produce blind spots as well!

It is worth considering that the seeds of Western modernity were planted in the late eleventh and twelfth centuries. Adnan Husain (2022) has called this period of history 'the formation of a crusading society'. During this period, multiple crusades were waged against Muslims, Jews, pagans, and others both in the East and the West, from the Levant to the Iberian Peninsula, on the basis that non-Christian-occupied land should be rightfully returned to Christian people. Crusaders understood Jerusalem to be the rightful home of the children of Christ. They also thought continental Europe was Christian land. After all, Christianity had become the official state religion of the Roman Empire once Constantine converted to Christianity in the early fourth century. The Christian Roman Empire then ruled over vast swaths of this territory. The first crusaders therefore marched to Jerusalem on the presumption that it was populated by people whom they had determined were responsible for the murder of Christ and did not belong in Europe. This view was a break from the past whereby Muslims, Jews, and Christians were able to live and practice their faith under Islamic rule in Europe.

Prior to these crusades, killing other human beings would normally have been considered sinful for Christians. However, during the crusades, Christian state power, or Christendom, began to sanction the murder of non-Christians if they failed to convert. This sanctioning of state violence against those deemed to be other is one of the key features of modernity.

Simultaneously, Franciscan and Dominican missionaries were commissioned to convert Jews, Muslims, and others deemed to be heretics. These missionaries sought martyrdom in the process. When missionaries failed at converting people–and they often did– irrational Jews and Muslims were blamed for believing in what was considered the faulty magic of Judaism and Islam. This attempt to use state power to regulate different genres of human life, forcing it to conform to a dominant norm, to convert and assimilate or face expulsion and death, is another key feature of power in modernity, what Michel Foucault called *governmentality* (see Burchell and Foucault 2009).

Through the crusades, new political forms of temporal and spatial knowledge began to emerge that were also key to the formation of the modern period. For example, a linear conception of history was established based on the providential view that God is in control of history and the endpoint of history is eternal salvation for those who seek redemption in Christ. This temporality has been fundamental to notions of linear progress in Western modernity, that all people and nations pass through the same stages of development towards an endpoint that is ever closer to truth, beauty, and justice. The epistemic framework of universalism that has been so fundamental to Western modernity was also established during this period. After all, Christendom began to see itself as responsible for all the world's people, and, with this responsibility, came the management of life and death to the edges of the mapped earth. From this point of view, Western Europeans began to imagine themselves as the universal figure of the human rather than, as Sylvia Wynter (2003) has put it, a *specific genre of being human* (295). New concepts of territoriality and borders also became significant. Amy Remensnyder, a historian of mediaeval Christianity, points out that the modern conceptual usage of the frontier first emerged through the crusadorial imaginary in the thirteenth century (2017, 100). The concept of the frontier, so central to later settler practices in the Americas and Israel, emerged to describe 'the space where the Christian polity touched its Islamic neighbour' on the Iberian Peninsula (Remensnyder 2017, 102). Intertwined with these new borders and frontiers were the classification, valuation, and spatialisation of human life. At this time, Christian maps, such as the Hereford Mappa Mundi (c. 1290–1300), began to depict Jewish and Muslim people 'on the fringes of the physical and moral world' as monsters and idolaters (Remensnyder 2017, 95). Christendom as a form of religious state power was therefore concerned with the rightful restoration of land to Christian control through ecclesiastically sanctioned displacement, conversion, and killing. Here, we begin to see the seeds of a nation-state form that is based on the expulsion or killing of those deemed to be foreign and inferior to the population of the state. We also begin to see how imperialist invasions of racialised populations in another part of the world gave shape and rise to the sense of a nation-state and its character at home. This doubleness of empire is another common refrain of Western modernity, one that echoes through each nativist assertion to expel those deemed to be foreign to the Western world from the Western world.

We also begin to see the seeds of how racialised populations are regulated bureaucratically based on dominant social norms. Medieval historian R.I. Moore (1987) noted how Christendom developed a centralised administrative approach to the classification, regulation, and subjugation of heretics, Jews, lepers, women prostitutes, and homosexual men. (He overlooked Muslims). Moore notes how administrative systems emerged during Christendom to manage these populations. For example, one system emerged to diagnose, classify, and record people with leprosy and then spatially segregate them by law. State power forced them to wear a costume and a bell so they could be identified and surveilled by sight and sound. They were also denied any social relations with families or friends. These surveillance instruments of power have been central to the state management of populations throughout the history of Western modernity (see Browne 2015; Foucault 1976). This short history of the crusades shows how they were key to the formation of knowledge and power that has been central to modernity. Through the crusades modernity emerges through developing state forms that regulate, expel, and kill racialised populations that are deemed to be fundamentally different in human character.

The next key moment in the beginnings of Western modernity is the year 1441, a year often overlooked in decolonial perspectives but not Black social and political thought. In 1441, Antão Gonçalves, a Portuguese explorer, went on an expedition around the coast of present-day Senegal and then returned to the Iberian Peninsula with captured Africans, gold dust, and ostrich eggs. This moment marked the beginning of crown-sanctioned raids on the West African coast to kidnap and traffic Black African people to Portugal. Approximately 1000 people from the West African coast were taken to Portugal between 1441 and 1448. This decade—the 1440 s—witnessed the European voyages that conquered territory on the coast of West Africa and is noted by Black studies scholars for its significance. Tiffany Lethabo King (2019), for example, argues that 1441 marks the 'inaugural time–space of the modern mode and era of conquest' (1). It is important therefore to mark the beginnings of Western modernity in the 1440 s and not simply begin with 1492. Otherwise, anti-Black racism can be downplayed as a key structuring force in Western modernity.

Another important date in the history of Western modernity is 1453. This year marks the fall or conquest of Constantinople—depending on who is telling the history and why. This moment is significant as it calls attention to Muslim resistance to Christian and Western state power. For critical Muslim studies scholars such as Salman Sayyid, this date is too easily overlooked in decolonial thought (see Sayyid 2014). Overlooking this important moment can lead to ahistorical analyses that only position Muslim people as, to use the Fanonian term, the 'wretched of the earth', or passive victims of Western modernity, rather than as people who have shaped the global history (Fanon 1965). Indeed, it was the growing influence of Islam in North Africa in the fifteenth century that led to key events in the year 1492, a year that is so significant to decolonial criticism from Latin American and Caribbean perspectives (Wynter 1995).

There are, in fact, multiple 1492 s (Stam and Shohat 2012). In January 1492, King Ferdinand and Queen Isabella, the monarchs of Catholic Spain, conquered the last Muslim state on the European continent in Granada, Spain. This campaign was stoked by fear of Islamic army invasion from North Africa to support this last remaining Muslim state. The expulsion of Muslim political power from Europe thus marked a key moment in which the European continent began to be identified as natively and purely Christian territory. The identification of Europe as Christendom was also shaped by decades of religious persecution known as the Spanish Inquisition. The Inquisition sought to identify heretics to the Catholic faith amongst those who converted to Catholicism from Judaism and Islam and resided within the Spanish Catholic ruled territories on the Iberian Peninsula. As early as 1478, Christian state power in Spain developed techniques for managing Muslim and Jewish populations: Muslim and Jewish people had to wear identifiable clothing, and open their homes on sacred days, so that their religious practices could be monitored. They were forced to eat pork publicly to break their own religious practices. People hung hams in their windows to show that they were not Jewish or Muslim, even if they practised their religions secretly to avoid arrest, torture, and possible death. Torture was used during this period to extraction confessions such as the use of water to induce a sensation of drowning alive and avoid leaving the traces of violence on bodies. The techniques and bureaucratisation of torture–the requirement of the presence of a doctor before torture, the documentation of confessions in official registers–have been transported through history, having eerie resonances with the legalisation and rationalisation of so-called 'enhanced interrogation methods' used by US armed forces on people racialised as Muslim who were captured and detained in prisons such as Abu Ghraib, Guantanamo, and Bagram under the banner of the War on Terror. The Spanish Inquisition culminated on 31 March 1492 with a royal decree that gave Jewish people the choice of conversion to Christianity, expulsion from Spain, or death.

Christopher Columbus had witnessed both historical events—the conquest of Al-Andalus and the Spanish Inquisition prior to setting sail for what he thought would be India on 3 August 1492. While voyaging to the Americas, Columbus addressed Ferdinand and Isabella in his logbook, noting how the conquest of Muslims and the expulsion of Jews from the Iberian Peninsula were inseparable in his mind from his nautical voyage. He wrote:

> On January 2 in the year 1492, when your Highnesses had concluded their the Moors who reigned in Europe, I saw your Highnesses' banners victoriously raised on the towers of the Alhambra, the citadel of that city, and the Moorish king come out of the city gates and kiss the hands of your Highnesses, and the prince, my Lord. And later in the same month... your Highnesses decided to send me Christopher Columbus, to see those parts of India and the princes and peoples of these lands, and consider the best means for their conversion... Therefore having expelled all the Jews from your domains in that same month of January, your Highness commanded me to go with an adequate fleet to those parts of India... I departed from the city of Granada on Saturday May 12 and went to the port of Palos, where I prepared three ships. (quoted in Armstrong 1992, 3)

This haunting passage points to the interconnection between the conquering of Muslims, the expulsion of Jews, and his voyage westward to the Americas. The global construction of religious difference and religious power on the European continent provides the foundation for the construction of racial and colonial differences throughout the world. A new global system based on European supremacy and centrality was about to begin.

When Columbus encountered Indigenous peoples in the Americas, he expressed an emerging racial ideology that was based on a nexus of religion and skin colour. Columbus sorted people into three racial categories—White, Black, and a colour that was, as he put it, 'neither black nor white' (quoted in Sweet 1997, 165). According to Columbus, the latter two groups were destined for servitude unlike those who were White; that is, Columbus articulated a ranking of human difference within a global system now shaped by racial power. His encounter with Indigenous people in the Americas stoked a multi-decade moral and theological debate in the Catholic Church on the European continent about the nature of Indigenous humanity and their entitlement to rights. In the infamous 'Valladolid Debate' (1550–1551), Bartolomé de las Casas and Juan Ginés de Sepúlveda argued whether Indigenous people belonged to the same human species or whether they were another creation. This question never needed to be asked, but it was. And the framing of the debate in those terms laid the foundations for the racialised world-system we inhabit today.

The global system that emerged in the long sixteenth century was predicated on creating racial dividing lines between those who were deemed to be human, less-than-human, or not human at all (see Weheliye 2014). These three divisions were shaped through a long history that began with the formation of a crusadorial society and culminated in the global projects of the Iberian Catholic monarchies that involved imperial conquest, territorial expulsion, slavery, and settler colonialism. Collectively, these projects targeted Jewish, Muslim, Black, and Indigenous people on multiple continents across the Atlantic Ocean. Of course, populations within this racial hierarchy were not targeted with the same techniques of subjugation in the early modern world. Other political and economic factors were in play. For example, Indigenous peoples in the Americas faced, and continue to face, elimination as a population because, according to Patrick Wolfe (2006), the primary Western European motive was (and remains) the occupation of Indigenous land. From his perspective, Indigenous presence and existence interferes with this settler colonial project. Indigenous people have faced the 'logic of elimination', Wolfe (2006) writes, through being 'killed, driven away, romanticised, assimilated, fenced in, bred White, and otherwise eliminated as the original owners of the land' (388). His view, which we have noted from the beginning, suggests that the motive underpinning the logic of elimination is the occupation of land.

An alternative view is that there is a constitutive relation in the modern/colonial world whereby those positioned as modern gain vitality and strength through elimination of populations that are deemed to impede, undermine, or threaten modernity, world vitality through the death of racialised and colonised others (Mbembe 2003). However, elimination has not been essential to other racial projects, such as transatlantic slavery (at least at first). In this case, enslaved populations needed to be kept alive and biologically reproduced–through brutal violence and coercive techniques of regulation–to maintain the viability of plantation-based economies in the Americas (see Weinbaum 2019). However, even in this instance, there were proposals for the abolition of slavery in the nineteenth century that proposed that the entire Black population in the US be eliminated through amalgamation, or state-planned racial intermixing (see Nyong'o 2009; Sexton 2008). From this perspective, the emerging racialised, colonial world-system developed a range of techniques, each with their own logic, to manage differently racialised populations to maintain and sustain this interconnected system.

In our tracing of the beginnings of modernity, there is a risk of placing too much emphasis on the Atlantic and Mediterranean Worlds. Cultural historians have long beckoned scholars to consider how South and East Asia became enfolded into this global system of Western racial power. Some analyses thus begin in the nineteenth century and focus on how the world's largest empire at that time, the British Empire, addressed labour shortages that arose from the abolition of slavery through managing the global migration of workers from the Asian continent (see Lowe 2015). However, there is a longer history to the incorporation of Asia into this global system. It, too, began in 1492 when the Portuguese empire conducted its first nautical exploration of the Indian Ocean and had begun to establish eastward maritime trade routes. In fact, it was the Portuguese eastward expansion that caused the competing Spanish empire to send Christopher Columbus westward in 1492 to find an alternative route to India. Upon disembarking in the Caribbean, he named the islands the 'Indies'. Prior to Columbus' journey in 1492, Portuguese ships were already travelling around the southern tip of Africa in 1488, reaching the Indian Ocean in 1498 and the Pacific Ocean in 1542. In the 1560 s, the Portuguese purchased enslaved Chinese people that Japanese pirates had kidnapped in coastal raids and sold in the ports of Japan. By 1500, the Portuguese had also already landed in present-day Brazil. By the mid-sixteenth century, the Portuguese empire had thus established what can be considered the first truly global network in history, one that linked the Americas, Africa, Europe, and Asia in an intricate exchange of goods and people—and, along with them, racial concepts and ideologies (Inglis 2011). Ever since, the emerging Western framework of human difference interacted with local epistemologies to become a deep force that has shaped and continues to shape the Western global system of racial power.

The *long history* of racial knowledge and power that we have been tracking above is absent within the tradition of critical race theory. As we have noted, critical race theory of education has focused on the persistence of racial disadvantage in education in the era following the American Civil Rights Movement in the 1960s, which legally abolished Jim Crow forms of segregation between Whites and Blacks. This perspective is strongly influenced by the view that 'race' and racism today does not operate in the same way that they did before the 1960s. From this perspective, racism before the 1960s in the US was overt whereas the racism after the 1960s is covert—but not less powerful (Bonilla-Silva 2010). This focus on the present, while important, risks ignoring how a global system of 'race' and racism existed prior to Jim Crow racism in the US and the emergence of nation-states in the seventeenth century. This racial, colonial system emerged through transnational grammars that compared, for example, the relative humanity of Christian people, Jewish people, Arab Muslim people, Black African people (who were also at times Muslim), Asian people, and Indigenous people, across multiple continents.

Taking this view, our approach to a global critical race perspective in education recognises a global continuity of 'race' and racism over a long millennium, with a particular emphasis on the significance of both the crusades and the long sixteenth century. Our perspective insists on studying 'race' and racism within national and local educational systems in relation to the global historical context of imperialism, colonialism, and slavery. Influenced by decolonial thought, our view recognises that the relations of power shaped through processes of racialisation have long outlived the formal end of non-settler colonial rule—a view that is captured by the term coloniality. According to Nelson Maldonado-Torres (2007), coloniality 'refers to long-standing patterns of power that emerged because of colonialism and which continue to define culture, labour, intersubjective relations, and knowledge production well beyond the strict limits of colonial administrations' (243). Importantly, as Ali

Meghji (2022) writes, the concept of coloniality 'links the historical events of colonialism with contemporary inequalities' (650). As such, coloniality emphasises 'a continuity between the past and the present (which) is well typified by how 'the West' has consistently positioned itself as being the epistemologically and materially dominant 'centre' of the globe even after the decolonisation of most of the world' (Meghji 2022, 650).

Through foregrounding the necropolitical concept of elimination, we are calling attention to the fact that Western modernity has bestowed strength, security, and vitality to the Western world through the destruction and death of racialised and colonised populations. This perspective is an important element in decolonial thought. In Ramón Grosfoguel's account of Western modernity, this global system has given a series of commands over the centuries to various populations:

"convert to Christianity or I'll kill you' in the 16th century ... 'civilise or I'll kill you' in the 18th and 19th centuries ... 'develop or I'll kill you' in the 20th century, and more recently ... 'democratise or I'll kill you' at the beginning of the 21st century'. (Grosfoguel 2012, 97)

While these colonial commands—convert, civilise, develop, or democratise—have changed throughout this long history, the other option—death—never has. Throughout this history, these commands have always been met with resistance and struggle. Indeed, that is the history of what Salman Sayyid (2014) calls 'the political', or the 'antagonism between friend and enemy' and the defining feature of this modern world (170). Indeed, the world-system was created through this racial antagonism and continues to be produced through this racial antagonism.

Perhaps, however, this vocabulary of antagonism is not strong enough to capture the sentiment expressed by Grosfoguel's tracing of modernity. Achille Mbembe (2003), the key thinker behind necropolitical thought, has described it as 'relation of enmity' rather than merely antagonism (12). For Mbembe, modernity is animated by a 'desire for an enemy, the desire for apartheid, for separation and enclosure, the phantasy of extermination' (2016, 23). From this vantage point, for example, the US did not invade Iraq with its allies in 2003 because it needed to secure its oil supply (the Marxian reading). It invaded Iraq because it had a desire for an enemy, for biophysical elimination, expressed in the command 'democratise or I'll kill you' (the decolonial reading). From this perspective, the Western sense of democracy is made through the targeting of populations that are deemed to lack the same capabilities for it. An education against elimination thus recognises that while racism has changed over time in various national contexts, a permanent feature of the nation-state is that it must explicitly kill the other to give life to those imagined as its people. And who is eliminated and why is shaped within a global system that values Whiteness and Europeanness as the standard bearer for humanity.

GLOBAL

Recognising the historical continuity of this global system of racial power points to new transnational directions for critical race perspectives in education. The dominant approach to critical race theory in educational studies has been to examine how local and national educational systems and practices contribute to reproducing racial advantages and disadvantages within localised boundaries. Sociologist Ali Meghji (2022, 651) has critiqued this tendency within critical race theory as an example of *methodological nationalism*. Methodological nationalism assumes that the modern nation-state is 'the natural social and political form of the modern world' (Wimmer and Glick Schiller 2002, 301), rather than, as we assume, that the nation-state is a colonial and racial apparatus that has been spread throughout the world through a long history of Western colonialism (Dragoş 2024, 5). Taking the nation-state as a natural social and political form, critical race theory of education has had the tendency to pick its unit of analysis as a national society and then look 'only within the spatial confines of that society, i.e. the confines of the particular nation-state' (Julian Go quoted in Meghji 2022, 651).

By contrast, through the long historical view presented in the previous section, it becomes easier to recognise how a racialised society has not existed independently from other racialised societies in the modern world. Moreover, it becomes easier to recognise how the nation-state itself is a racial state that seeks to establish purity within the nation—indeed, to establish the very idea of the nation and its imagined community—through the regulation, expulsion, and death of racialised populations (Goldberg 2002). This phenomenon can be observed in diverse examples from the liberal democratic Indian nation-state to the communist Chinese nation-state and their shared subjection of Muslim people. The modern nation-state, no matter its political form, can strengthen their position within a global economy of Whiteness through the regulation, expulsion, and killing of people racialised, for example, as Muslim, Black, and Indigenous. This orientation to the nation-state invites us to make transnational linkages that explain how educational systems and practices maintain and sustain this global racial order in interconnected ways. Through this interactional approach, a global critical perspective seeks to make connections between how 'race' and racism operates through education within established boundaries of a social system, such as the nation, in ways that connect with the operation of 'race' and racism outside those boundaries in other contexts.

This interactional and multi-scalar approach to 'race' and racism in education challenges conventional and critical approaches to the question of the global in education studies. Since the 1990s, the concept of *globalisation* has tended to be used to refer to how new innovations, particularly in digital technology and transportation, have increased and intensified the mobility and interconnectivity of goods, services, and people across the world. This interconnectivity has compressed time and space—meaning that goods, services, and people can travel further distances in a shorter time—on a pace and scale that had never been witnessed before in human history. Globalisation has also referred to the global spread of ideas and values, as well as cultural forms such as music and fashion.

This contemporary orientation to globalisation has shaped understandings of the greatest challenges before national education systems. Over the past few decades, educational reforms within countries have been promoted on the basis that they are competing with one another in this interconnected global economy in ever more intensified ways. Children and young people must now be prepared for international competition in labour markets where workers, jobs, and industries shift globally. To do so, they must develop broad skills that prepare them to adapt to structural shifts in labour marketplaces, as well as develop specific skills tailored to each nation's competitive market advantage. Science, technology, engineering, and mathematics (STEM) are prioritised in the curriculum because they are seen as most relevant to developing such skills. In the past, Western education systems valued the humanities for preparing their citizens to bear rights and responsibilities in liberal democracies (i.e. 'a liberal arts education'). The humanities developed both tolerance and taste fit for the liberal democratic subjects. Now, the humanities, if they are valued, are expected to develop cultural competencies that help people navigate human diversity in this globalised world.

The problem with this analysis of globalisation in education is that it is both race-avoidant and ahistorical, without any consideration of the antagonisms, or relations of enmity, at the heart of a global system shaped by 'race' and racism. Globalisation is not a new phenomenon. Of course, the world is interconnected in ways that it has never been before. But, as the analysis above shows, that is not to say that the world was not interconnected before. What has always been at the heart of this interconnected world is the construction and ranking of human difference, with Western Europeans nominating themselves as the superior genre of the human responsible for shaping the world's history. This world emerged in the long sixteenth century when Europeans started to imagine a non-European world incapable of bearing that same responsibility because: they lacked Christianity in the fifteenth and sixteenth centuries; rationality in the seventeenth and eighteenth centuries; the biological substance of Whiteness in the nineteenth and twentieth centuries; and, the culture of Whiteness in the twentieth and twenty-first centuries.

Decolonial scholars recognise this long global history of the world through the concept of the *modern/colonial world-system* (Mignolo 2000). This key concept has two important elements. The first element is the phrase modern/colonial. This phrase denotes the belief that the modern world emerged, as we began to address above, in the long sixteenth century through a relationship with the colonial world. The two entities—the modern world and the colonial world—are based on a mutually constitutive relation rather than a derivative one. In other words, the colonial world does not derive from the modern world. Instead, the modern world was established through making and targeting the colonial world. This interdependence is represented by the backslash punctuation mark ('/')'. This modern/colonial relation of difference constructed a social reality, a relation of enmity, in which the colonial world must be conquered and developed for the benefit of this modern world, even if that means its racialised inhabitants and its natural elements were to be eliminated and destroyed.

The second element in this decolonial concept of the modern/colonial world-system is the term *world-system* itself. This term originated through twentieth-century intellectual developments in Marxist theory (see Wallerstein 2004). These developments were born out of a scepticism towards studies that treated 'the nation' as a natural and contained unit of analysis (see discussion of *methodological nationalism* above). From a world-systems perspective, nation-states have always been and always continue to be in relation with other nation-states. Nation-states are connected through this history of the modern/colonial world because they emerged through managing these modern/colonial differences. This world-systems perspective also holds that the modern world established itself as 'the center of world history' (Dussel 2000, 470). By contrast, the colonial world was deemed to be peripheral to the center of world history. Peripheral does not mean a geographic location, but rather a subordinated one within a global system of power. Those people, places, regions, and nations that are peripheral are deemed to lag in this world history and dependent upon the modern world for shaping world history. In this way, the modern/colonial world-system describes how 'the whole planet became the space of one world history' with this center/peripheral, dominant/subordinate, historically mature/immature relations as its endemic feature (Dussel 2000, 470).

There is a strong relation between the concept of the modern/colonial world-system and the racial state. In the modern world, the colonial and cultural, not biological, designation between Europeanness and non-Europeanness has been a dominant feature of the modern-colonial world-system. In this way, individuals, populations, and nation-states are racialised as being European, non-European, or proximate to Europeanness. In the modern-colonial world-system, there is thought to be one pathway of development, one telos, whereby all the world's people and their nations must progress from non-Europeanness to Europeanness for the betterment of humanity. How does this happen? It happens through the regulation, expulsion, and death of populations that are deemed to be a hindrance or threat to that teleological imperative. For this very reason, nation-states throughout the world today regulate, expel, or kill populations that are deemed to be too Muslim, too Black, and too Native. Such moves face little resistance from the Western world when they exercise this biopolitical and necropolitical power. In the modern/colonial world-system, nation-states strengthen their position within a matrix of power through doing so.

The term modern/colonial world-system thus brings together these two ideas: the interdependence of nation-states (world-system) and uneven relations of power across the globe (modern/colonial). This global orientation offers a challenge to conventional approaches in educational studies to critical race theory that have sought to apply this perspective outside of the US context. When this analytical move has been done, the concern has often been about how this theoretical perspective might be translated from the US context to another local or national context (Goodnight 2017). *Theoretical translation* is 'the act of translating a theoretical framework from its original context to another place for the purpose of conducting and interpreting social research' (Goodnight 2017, 665). Critical race theory has been translated for non-US educational contexts, from India in the Global South to the UK in the Global North (Goodnight 2017; Warmington 2020). However, the concept of the modern/colonial world-system suggests that the challenge is not necessarily to translate this theoretical framework from one national context to another. The challenge is to explain how local and national educational systems are interconnected in maintaining and sustaining a global racial order.

Indeed, this concept of the modern/colonial world-system has not yet had a strong impact on critical race theory in educational studies (Meghji 2022). The modern/colonial world-system concept makes it clear that 'race' and racism preceded the emergence of liberal democratic states in the eighteenth century. Moreover, 'race' and racism impact modern nation-states today that are neither liberal nor democratic. The reason is because nation-states are not only interlinked today in this modern/colonial world-system, but also that the nation-state as a racial and colonial apparatus was exported throughout the world through Western colonisation and has always been interlinked in this modern/colonial world-system. As a result, this global critical perspective provides an orientation towards establishing the workings of 'race' and racism both within and across nation-states. This transnational orientation is necessary to imagine and enact other worlds free from the threat posed to life through racial domination.

THE RACIAL POLITICS OF PROPERTY AND BEING

So many students that we teach today who are interested in decolonial and anti-racist education do not see value in critical race theory. They are hesitant to engage with this scholarly conversation because critical race theory so often frames 'race' and racism in the American context. Within this context, 'race' is often reduced to colour through references to a White-Black racial dualism that has shaped racial conflict in the US since the nation's founding. Moreover, critical race theory has tended to approach 'race' and racism in juridical and political terms. Recognising that 'race' has no biological or material reality, critical race theory has argued that 'race' is continuously produced in America through a legal system that rules who is White (or not) and whether someone is being treated equally because they are White or not. 'Race' is continually produced through a political system that uses census tools to count who is White or not, and legislating advantages or disadvantages that might arise from being counted as White or not.

From this juridical and political orientation, Cheryl Harris (1993) put forward the compelling idea that Whiteness should be seen as a form of property. In other words, Whiteness is framed as a possession that exists outside of people that they can then have or own—like a piece of land or a building or an investment. Whiteness has value that yields rewards so everyone, no matter whether they are White or not, should want to have it. Indeed, Harris (1993) argued that the American legal system established Whiteness as 'the quintessential property for personhood', one that entitled individuals to political rights and economically valuable benefits (p. 1730). Throughout its history, various racial groups have fought before the American legal system over whether they are White to gain those same rights and benefits. Repeatedly, this American legal system, critical race theorists have argued, has protected Whiteness as a form of property through excluding people racialised as non-White so that they are unable to enjoy them.

Whiteness as property strongly influenced critical race theory of education in its earliest inception. In their seminal paper, Gloria Ladson-Billings and William Tate (1995) point to the various ways in which Whiteness as property is germane to educational analysis. For example, one of the fundamental characteristics of property is its transferability, or *alienability* (Ladson-Billings and Tate IV 1995, 59). Whiteness can be transferred to students who are racialised as non-White when they are rewarded 'for conformity to perceived 'white norms' or sanctioned for cultural practices', such as dress or speech patterns (Ladson-Billings and Tate IV 1995, 59). A second characteristic of property is that it includes the *right of use and enjoyment* (Ladson-Billings and Tate IV 1995, 59). Educational systems and institutions protect Whiteness when they establish material differences between what students from different racial groups can use and enjoy, from facilities to textbooks (Ladson-Billings and Tate IV 1995, 59). A third characteristic of property is that it comes with symbolic meaning, or with *reputation and status* (Ladson-Billings and Tate IV 1995, 60). An American school system or institution labelled 'urban' or 'Black' has its relative reputational value and status diminished

(Ladson-Billings and Tate IV 1995, 60). A fourth and final character-istic of property is its *right to exclude* (Ladson-Billings and Tate IV 1995, 60). After all, African-American children were historically segre-gated from schools attended by White children. After this segregation was deemed unconstitutional in the 1950s, White families fled cities for suburban schools and private schools, as well as established gifted and talented programmes within public schools, to continue these exclu-sionary practices (Ladson-Billings and Tate IV 1995, 60). In these various ways, US educational systems and practices have been deeply implicated in protecting Whiteness as a form of property, which, in turn, provides material advantages to those who benefit within this system from being racialised as White.

This framing of Whiteness as a form of property arose through critical race theory's deep suspicion of liberalism. This political philosophy was the primary force in shaping the American legal system and its rule of law from the nation's inception. David Graeber (2014) argued that liberalism is 'a tradition that assumes that liberty is essentially the right to do what one likes with one's own property. In fact, not only does it make property a right, it treats rights themselves as a form of property' (205). In this way, liberalism conceptualises liberties as properties that people possess. People are thought to *have* liberties, such as the freedom of speech or freedom of assembly. The alternative view is that liberties are a relation. My freedom to speak my mind is never separate from another person's choice to not hurt me for doing so. Thinking of liberties as possessions rather than rela-tions means that liberties become alienable. They can be taken, bought, and sold. This point is important because liberalism emerged historically at the same time as Western European imperialism and slavery. If liberty was a possession, then those conquered in war could legally have their liberty taken from them through enslavement (the juridical defence of slavery) and those deemed to be racially inferior could have their liberty taken from them through enslavement (the racial defence of slavery). In the history of the US, the racial defence of slavery was enshrined into law with the founding of the US constitution, and in so doing, estab-lished Whiteness in the US as a 'race' with value. After all, the property of Whiteness came with liberties that were not granted to other racial groups. For this reason, critical race theory has called attention to the juridical framing of Whiteness as a form of property. This framing has influenced those education scholars who adopted this legal framework to study how American educational systems and practices sustain the value of Whiteness over time.

While framing Whiteness as a form of property can be useful in contexts in and outside the US (see Wang and Denmead 2025), it is not always helpful in understanding how racism operates both within and beyond the US. To put it crudely, the genocide in Gaza cannot be adequately explained through the lens of protecting Whiteness as a form of property that has the right, for example, to exclude people from the same rewards and opportunities. The genocide in Gaza can only be explained through seeing 'racism' as a force with the desire and the power to preserve some genres of life and eliminate other genres of life. For this very reason, decolonial thought from Latin American and Caribbean contexts avoids addressing 'race' and racism through the symbolics of property. These scholars also do not approach the world as one that is divided by colour. They instead address 'race' and racism through the symbolics of the human.

For example, drawing on anti-colonial thought of Frantz Fanon (2008), Ramón Grosfoguel (2016) argues that 'racism is a global hierarchy of superiority and inferiority along the line of the human' (10). From this vantage point, the history of 'race' and racism begins in the long sixteenth century when Western Europeans began to *overrepresent* themselves, as Sylvia Wynter (2003) argued, as the form of the human through a relation with those who do not rise to the same level of humanness. They are projected into a realm of otherness. This orientation shifts the attention from what we might call the *racial politics of property* to the *racial politics of being* in the modern world (Wynter 2003, 318). This attention on the racial politics of being is fundamental because it draws attention to what is so often politically at stake with 'race' and racism: life and death, preservation and elimination of cultures, state protection and state terror.

From this perspective, Whiteness should not merely be understood as a form of property within liberal democratic nation-states. Whiteness should be understood as the 'genre of the human' that has been afforded the dominant racial position within the modern/colonial world in relation to people constructed as those who lack this same humanity, or any humanity at all (Wynter 2003, 317). This conception of Whiteness recognises that the history of Whiteness precedes biological and scientific conceptions of 'race' in the nineteenth century. As a result, Whiteness, and any other 'race', is not reducible to skin colour or anything biological in nature. Instead, the roots of 'race' can be found in various colonial distinctions that have been made from the sixteenth century onwards between 'peoples (nations/tribes), identities (Christians/pagans), ecologies (landscapes/wildernesses), cultures (civilised/savage), histories (progressive/arrested), corporealities (superior/inferior)' (Hesse 2007, 659). These colonial markers of racial difference have become inscribed in language and relations of power. The dominant position is White/European and the subordinate position is non-White/non-European.

This perspective can make it difficult to see how and when populations are being racialised within a global system of racial power if colour is not always a reliable marker of 'race'. Indeed, we made this point clear in the introduction as we sought to make a connection between the various threats to those racialised as Muslim in the occupied territories of Palestine, Myanmar, Kashmir, and Western China. How does one determine whether populations are being racialised and subjected to racial power if 'colour' is not only how racialisation operates? W.E.B. Du Bois offered a powerful example that helps illustrate how to answer this question. Du Bois recognised that Blackness has no material or biological reality and that skin colour itself was not a reliable indicator of an individual's identity or social position as a Black person. Without a reliable referent, Du Bois (1940) stated that he could recognise Blackness because 'the black man is a person who must ride 'Jim Crow' in Georgia' (77). In other words, Du Bois argued that what makes a person identifiable in terms of 'race' is not a physical marker per se, but rather a structural position within a system of racial power. Through the lens of the White-Black racial binary, a person is made Black when they are made to ride in a segregated and demarcated portion of the train car. A person is made White when they are permitted to travel in whatever train car they please. These racialised positions are maintained and sustained over time through a process of contestation, making them structural positions within a system of racial power. People learn to act in ways that are associated with the positions they have inherited.

This same logic applies to the racial distinction between those who are deemed to be above the line of the human and those who are deemed to be below the line of the human. Colour is not always a reliable indicator of this distinction. What is a reliable indicator of this distinction is whether a population is being targeted with extreme forms of violence. What does this extreme form of violence look like? In his paper introducing necropower, Achille Mbembe (2003) provided this horrific portrait:

> fortified structures, military posts, and roadblocks everywhere; buildings that bring back painful memories of humiliation, interrogations, and beatings; curfews that imprison hundreds of thousands in their cramped homes every night from dusk to daybreak; soldiers patrolling the unlit streets, frightened by their own shadows; children blinded by rubber bullets; parents shamed and beaten in front of their families; soldiers urinating on fences, shooting at the rooftop water tanks just for fun, chanting loud offensive slogans, pounding on fragile tin doors to frighten the children, confiscating papers, or dumping garbage in the middle of a residential neighborhood; border guards kicking over a vegetable stand or closing borders at whim; bones broken; shootings and fatalities. (39)

He left out sexual violence from sexual humiliation to rape. Amidst this violence, the naturalised and legitimised pathway carved out in this racial system for racially subordinated people to gain sovereignty over their own lives, to avoid this *death-world*, is to attempt to become more proximate to the White/European position (Mbembe 2003, 40). The illegitimate pathway, the one that is met with ever more violence, is resistance and opposition.

Throughout the history of the modern world, education has been held out as one pathway to escape these death-worlds. In colonial regimes, education is understood as a mechanism through which colonised populations can acquire the norms, values, and beliefs of the coloniser's civilised culture. From this point of view, colonised populations are deemed to be 'educable' unlike other racialised populations that are deemed to be 'ineducable' (see Denmead et al. 2024). Colonised people become ready for self-governance and national independence if they acquire that civilised culture and become more historically mature through education. They become ready for self-governance and national independence if their own native culture is eliminated. This is a *colonial relation* (Mielants and Grosfoguel 2006, 3). This colonial relation is key to the formation of the nation-state as a political form. Through the history of the modern world, the nation-state as a political form was deemed to be available to those who were 'educated' in the modern world and not yet available to those who were only 'educable' in the colonial world. Those in countries outside the West were deemed to not yet be entitled to political sovereignty because their people had not yet acquired sufficient European character.

This same racial and colonial logic is pervasive today, an assumption rooted in the concept of *coloniality of being* (Maldonado-Torres 2007). The coloniality of being plays a role in shaping how nations and territories, and people within nations and territories, are understood as superior and inferior, dominant and subordinate, rational and irrational, historically mature and historically immature, culturally underdeveloped and culturally developed. For this very reason, education is still entangled in the production of this global racial order because it is imagined as a mechanism through which formerly colonised people can develop along this singular line of development towards Whiteness and Europeanness, and once they achieve it, they will be more capable of exercising sovereignty over their own lives. However, this colonial relation means that those nations and people deemed to be beneath and outside the dividing line of Whiteness and Europeanness are in a perpetual state of always trying to catch up to them. They are always positioned as those who must accomplish what those states and individuals have already accomplished: technological progress, productive capacity, and rational government (see Nguyen 2012, 16–17).

This decolonial perspective on 'race' and racism allows us to recognise a global racial hierarchy of regions and countries and the role of education in maintaining and sustaining it. Countries are often imagined in homogenous racial terms based on the racial classification of 'the people' who are presumed to define the character of the nation. For example, the US is so often framed ideologically as a White nation because the character of the nation is assumed to be White. This racial identification of a nation is not fixed. For example, South Africa may have been framed as a White nation before apartheid was ended in 1991 whereas post-apartheid South Africa was defined as a Black nation. Throughout this history of South Africa, the White population has remained the small minority of the country (8–11 per cent). Social meanings are also continuously assigned to a nation based on this ascribed racial character of the nation. Nations are then placed in a global racial order based on those meanings. Through this process, countries and regions, like people, compete in a global system of racial and colonial power for rewards that are bestowed on them with respect to their greater proximity to Europeanness and Whiteness.

This perspective thus explains how and why this modern/colonial world is maintained and sustained. Groups within nations, and nations themselves, seek to occupy a position that historically has been associated with humanity because that position provides greater autonomy, greater life chances, and greater freedom from routine forms of extreme violence. As we have argued throughout this book, nations can attempt to occupy that position through the literal or cultural elimination of racially and colonially subordinated populations that are deemed to be a threat to this global system of White domination. Today, populations made most vulnerable to this violence in the name of catching up to modernity vary across contexts, but are often Black, Muslim, or Latin American. This framework helps explain, for example, how the nation of India today is exercising racial power against Muslim people (see Kattiparambil 2024). Muslim people are being subjected to racial violence with relative impunity from other nations because the Muslim subject is deemed to be a threat to a global system of White domination based on their ascribed irrationality, barbarity, superstition, and transnational political affiliation with a worldwide community of Islamic believers ('Ummah'). While the White (or Anglo-Indian) population is small in India, this racial violence towards Muslim people becomes one way for the nation to follow a linear Western path towards a more dominant position within a global system of White domination. India can attempt to catch up to the modern position through regulating, expelling, and eliminating Muslim people from its borders. At first glance, this example may not seem like a 'race' matter because both groups of people might be 'dark-skinned'. But, as we have written throughout this book, that is not how 'race' and racism operates. It often operates through cultural difference, which, in this case, is religious in nature.

That said, culture is not always a reliable indicator of 'race' and racism either. As Salman Sayyid pointed out at the 2025 Critical Muslim Studies Conference in Istanbul ('Summer Programme - Critical Muslim Studies' 2025), one of the first individuals killed in the US by an overt racist person in retaliation for the 9/11 attacks was Balbir Singh Sodhi. Sodhi was a Sikh man who was mistaken for a Muslim person ('Murder of Balbir Singh Sodhi' 2025). This example illustrates how a person may be racialised as a particular 'race'—in this case, as a Muslim—even though they are, in fact, not members of that 'race'. The same can be said for Palestinian Christians in Gaza. In the early days of Israel's 2023 bombardment of Gaza, the Israeli state killed 18 Christians who were seeking safety in a Greek Orthodox Catholic church ('Church of Saint Porphyrius Airstrike' 2025). While the Israeli state would likely argue that this outcome was collateral damage, or unintended harm, the fact of the matter is that the bombs that killed them were targeting Muslims. The bombs never would have been dropped if they were targeting Christians. So, whether the bombs were intended to kill Christians, these Christians were killed by being positioned and targeted as Muslims. In this way, a global critical race perspective of education must continuously pay attention to the elastic and expansive ways in which people are racialised as members of a particular group in ways that make no sense but are still deadly all the same. 'Race' and racism never makes sense, and it does not have to (Razack 2022).

Critical race theory has provided powerful ways of thinking about Whiteness as a form of property. The racial politics of property focuses attention on segregation and exclusion, as well as material advantages and disadvantages, that are contested within a liberal system of governance. However, property is too limiting as a framework for understanding how 'race' and racism threatens life and ways of being. A decolonial perspective on 'race' and racism is therefore crucial to a global critical race perspective on education. The racial politics of being focuses attention on elimination within a global system of modern/colonial governance. Given the abhorrent and non-exceptional nature of racial violence in the modern world, a global perspective on 'race' and racism must be attuned to the racial politics of being as much as the racial politics of property.

LEARNING WHITENESS ON A GLOBAL SCALE

A fundamental assumption in this book is that this global system of White domination is neither natural nor inevitable. Rather, this system is one that is 'forged and sustained through specific and ongoing practices of colonial violence and racial injustice' (Sriprakash, Rudolph, and Gerrard 2022, 4). As we have argued throughout this book, education is deeply implicated in the reproduction of this global system because people throughout the world learn to act in ways that either preserve or contest it. This process of learning is more often subtle and slow, rather than intentional and obvious. People can learn racially motivated behaviour without necessarily developing prejudicial attitudes towards others. Rather people develop racial interests within a racialised system that distributes advantages and disadvantages, including life and death, unevenly across racial hierarchies at both national and global scales. The racialised global system that we have inherited is one that rewards Whiteness as a structural position of racial power because of its associations with vitality, advancement, progress, intelligence, beauty, wealth, taste, and civilisation. In this sense, this global system of White domination is maintained and sustained when people learn that Whiteness is exclusively associated with these virtues, and that it is natural and inevitable that rewards are bestowed upon those positioned as White for that very reason.

From this vantage point, Whiteness is fundamentally an educational concern because it is learned. As Arathi Sriprakash, Sophie Rudolph, and Jessica Gerrard (2022) argue in their book *Learning Whiteness*, 'lessons in Whiteness make and sustain global colonial and capitalist orders, seeking to normalise and relay racialised hierarchies within and across states' (4). In this short passage, the authors make clear that racialised hierarchies that privilege Whiteness, and make that privilege appear normal and natural, operate at both local/national and global scales. Indeed, the two interact with one another. For example, the racialised hierarchy that is structuring the genocide in Gaza is not merely a question of local identity—Israelis and Palestinians. The racialised hierarchy in question is European-Jewish-White and non-European-Brown-Muslim. While there is a distinct and locally specific relation between 'races' in this context, this relation interacts with a global racial structure. Indeed, this local process of racialisation interacts with racialisation at a global scale that imagines the nation of Israel as a civilised Western outpost amidst the barbarity of the Middle East. This example illustrates how racialised hierarchies are normalised within and across borders, territories, and states.

This important perspective turns our attention on the ways in which *Global Whiteness* is made and learned. This concept of Global Whiteness refers explicitly to the dominant structural position of Whiteness within a global system of racial power (Christian 2019). From this perspective, people, regions, and nations are racialised within a global system of racial power, and various advantages and disadvantages, including the freedom from extreme violence, are distributed unevenly across this hierarchy. People throughout the world learn to act in ways that either preserve or contest this global system of racial power for themselves and their territories and nations depending on their relative position, and their nation's position, within this global system. Within this framework, learning *Global Whiteness* means:

1. learning that Whiteness is a desirable position for regions and nations throughout the world to occupy precisely because it comes with existential, symbolic, and material rewards.
2. nations and regions adopting values, beliefs, norms, customs, practices, and knowledge that have been historically associated with, and privileged, this dominant position.
3. learning how to explain that those existential, symbolic, and material rewards distributed unevenly to nations and regions within a global system of racial domination are natural and justified.

In this way, learning Global Whiteness seeks to normalise and relay racialised hierarchies within, across, and between regions and nations. Education becomes a key mechanism in this teaching and learning, and therefore becomes implicated in the reproduction and contestation of this global system of White domination over time.

It is necessary to pay attention to how Whiteness is learned at the micro-levels of groups and individuals within regions, territories, and nation-states and how this learning interacts with reproducing a global racialised hierarchy of nation-states. Given its colonial and Western roots, this global racialised hierarchy places countries and regions such as the US, Canada, Western Europe, and Australia in the dominant position of the world-system and countries in Africa and South Asia are positioned in the subordinate position. Other countries and regions from Eastern Europe, South America, and Gulf states are placed in a liminal position between these two poles. This global system is reproduced as people within regions and nations, and regions and nations themselves, adopt practices and policies that preserve and protect the global structural position of Whiteness. For those people, regions, and nations in liminal spaces within this global structure, the process of attempting to become more proximate to Whiteness as a population or a nation has been referred to as amalgamation or *whitening* (see, for example, Viveros Vigoya 2015).

Western colonial empires developed explicit strategies to whiten colonised populations both culturally and phenotypically through racial intermixing, colonial education, and systematically exterminating Black and Indigenous populations. These three strategies operated within and across generations to fundamentally change the ascribed racial character of nations. The persistence of whitening after the formal end of external colonial rule is an example of coloniality. Brazil, for example, adopted formal state policies to whiten the population through intermixing and education in the early twentieth century. This policy was aimed at forging a new Brazilian White national identity that was more proximate to a European White identity. This example shows the strong link between racial and national identities within a global system of racial power. While a formal policy to whiten a nation's population may no longer be enacted, whitening remains as a strategy for people and nations to achieve a better existence within a global system of racial power (Viveros Vigoya 2015). Whitening can be a difficult concept to work with analytically because it can lead to accusations that 'whitened' individuals have betrayed their authentic racial identity. This accusation against individuals is problematic because there is no essence to 'race' and there are endlessly varied ways in which people can perform their racial identities. The problem is with those in a dominant position who fiercely protect their advantages within this system, and, in turn, establish whitening as a phenomenon.

Education is implicated in this coloniality of whitening. It can act as one of the key cultural mechanisms through which a nation might attempt to position itself as one that possesses the markers of Europeanness and Whiteness. Examples might include learning English, adopting individualism, consumption, and accumulation as cultural norms, acquiring higher education degrees from institutions in the US and the UK. However, no matter how much a population historically racialised as non-White within this global system may adopt practices such as these, these populations will always be positioned as those that are trying to catch up temporally to Whiteness—that is, to be positioned as modern as Whiteness. Whiteness operates by always positioning itself as the most temporally advanced, most modern position of power in the world (Denmead 2021). As a result, any group racialised as non-White will always be positioned as behind and inferior to Whiteness no matter how much whitening occurs. Whitening as a strategy thus contributes to reproducing the modern-colonial world by reasserting the dominant structural position of Whiteness within a global racial hierarchy.

Of course, some will argue that the rise in power of non-European nations that are racialised as non-White signals the decline, perhaps even the end, of this global system. This perspective has become more common as, for example, countries such as China, India, and Brazil have become more dominant in the global sphere. The rise of these nations might suggest that, for example, Whiteness does not have the same value or power as it once had. The alternative view is that racialised hierarchies within nations are reproduced as dominant groups compete for the symbolic and social status of Whiteness on a global scale (Christian 2019, 180). In other words, a dominant social group in a country that is racialised as non-White and positioned beneath Western White nations, such as Han Chinese in China, high-caste Indians in India, and White Brazilians in Brazil, may attempt to gain to proximity to Whiteness and White spaces in order to reproduce their dominance at national scale. The rise of non-Western international students in Western education systems is one indication of this phenomenon. Seeking international educational opportunities is shaped by various meanings attached to Whiteness, including, for example, reason and intelligence. This whitening of dominant groups within nations through education thus maintains and sustains this system of White domination on a global scale. From this perspective, Whiteness is neither losing its value nor position of dominance. Instead, Whiteness on a global scale structures the racial ordering (and educational outcomes) within nation-states.

A global critical race perspective recognises that Whiteness as a structural position within a global system of racial power is learned. Whiteness must be learned because whiteness belongs to the social world, not the natural world. How then does this learning occur? Both knowledge and emotions are integral aspects of learning. We learn how to think and what to think, how to feel and what to feel, in ways that shape how we act. Within a system of racial power, we learn how to think and what to think, how to feel and what to feel, in ways that shape how we act towards conserving or contesting this system of racial power. We therefore turn to the role of knowledge and emotions in learning Whiteness within a global system of White domination.

Knowledge

Educational systems are foremost concerned with the pursuit, production, and dissemination of knowledge. The dominant tendency in education is to think of this pursuit, production, and dissemination of knowledge as an apolitical and neutral project. This view holds that knowledge is 'out there' in the world, waiting to be discovered, and then once discovered, is passed along to others through education for the benefit of human flourishing and progress. However, critical perspectives take the view that the pursuit, production, and dissemination of knowledge is always implicated in maintaining and sustaining particular social orders rooted in power, including racial ones. There is a nexus between power and knowledge

(Foucault and Gordon 1980). This nexus between knowledge and power arises in a variety of ways:

- Some knowledge is *pursued* whereas other knowledge is *ignored*.
- Some knowledge is *produced* whereas other knowledge is *concealed*.
- Some knowledge is *disseminated* whereas other knowledge is *erased* or *destroyed*.

From this vantage point, knowledge that is pursued, produced, or disseminated versus knowledge that is ignored, concealed, or destroyed is always tied to some political interest. Some groups will benefit materially, if not existentially, and other groups will be harmed from the dissemination of dominant knowledge and the concealment of oppositional knowledge. Some groups will benefit, and other groups will be harmed from the dissemination of dominant knowledge and the non-dissemination of oppositional knowledge. Some groups will benefit, and others will be harmed through the destruction of systems, such as universities and libraries, that are necessary for producing knowledge. Societies that are structured in relations of dominance therefore inevitably struggle through the *politics of knowledge* (Said 2013). In this section, we review some of the basic educational concepts associated with not only the politics of knowledge, but also the *politics of cognition*. However, we point out that an approach to education against elimination must necessarily be attuned to the intimate relationship between knowledge and violence, a relationship that is foregrounded in post-colonial and decolonial thought.

Given the strong relationship between education and knowledge, educationists must always engage critically with whose interests are served by pursuing, producing, and disseminating some knowledge and ignoring, concealing, and destroying other knowledge. The politics of knowledge shape how people think and provide them tools for understanding the social reality that they experience. Depending on one's position within a society structured in dominance, people will be more likely to learn to think and will be more likely to understand the reality that they experience, in ways that will benefit and protect their interests. These tendencies will be shared within groups, and these groups will in turn act in ways that are largely informed by this way of thinking, by this understanding of social reality. That said, there always remains scope (and hope!) for people to learn and think differently than their structural position might determine. If positions of dominance are learned, they can be unlearned. Nonetheless, the long history of modernity indicates that unlearning positions of dominance does not occur without a struggle from those in subordinate positions and their allies calling for justice.

Politics of cognition matter as much as the politics of knowledge to critical educational analyses. These two concepts are slightly different. After all, the reproduction of a system structured in racial domination is not merely a question of what people know or do not know (politics of knowledge). It is also a question of how people think or do not think (politics of cognition). The dominant tendency within educational studies is to assume that educational actors, such as principals and teachers, are acting rationally when they teach and that students learn to think rationally through learning from them in classrooms and other settings. Critical educational perspectives, however, draw attention to how education can also teach irrational processes of cognition to maintain systems of power. Indeed, this focus on cognition and power is fundamental to Marxist orientations to educational thought. This tradition has emphasised how people experience *mystification* through education. Through education, people learn ways of thinking that prevent them from seeing the world as it really is. From a Marxist standpoint, educational systems, institutions, and classrooms conceal the relationship of domination and subordination within capitalism, and indeed, make that relationship look natural, thus enabling this relationship of dominance to be conserved rather than contested. From this vantage point, people develop a *false consciousness* and a critical pedagogy counteracts this falseness through attempting to cultivate a *critical consciousness* (Freire 2000). However, this approach has been criticised for the ways in which students are often, paradoxically, positioned as those who have not yet developed a critical consciousness, and are therefore dependent upon someone more knowledgeable and powerful than them—namely, teachers and academics (see Ellsworth 1989). From this vantage point, the teachers are often positioned as those who can see the real. However, the reality is that students bring critical vantage points that teachers in positions of power can sometimes lack.

This politics of cognition has been a key debate in structural theories of 'race' and racism (see Mueller 2020). One of the major concepts that explains the relationship between individual cognition and the reproduction of the racial order is *racial ideology*. Ideologies, or 'meaning in the service of power', is a concept associated with Marxism (Bonilla-Silva 2022, 80). However, structural racism theory adapts this concept to explain racism. From this vantage point, racial ideology refers to meanings in service of racial power. A racial ideology provides framings and stories of racial problems that express 'as 'common sense' the interests of the dominant race, while oppositional ideologies attempt to challenge that common sense by providing alternative frames, ideas, and stories based on the experiences of subordinated races' (Bonilla-Silva 2022, 10). A racial ideology helps people make sense of racial matters in ways that justify or challenge the existing racial order.

Critical race theory has largely attacked the dominant racial ideology in Western liberal and democratic societies, that of *color-blind racism* (Bonilla-Silva 2022) (see Fig. 2). Colour-blind racism is based on the liberal belief that Western democratic societies must (and largely do) treat people equally no matter their race. From this vantage point, differences in social outcomes for racial groups are the fair and legitimate outcome of a meritocratic process, not a rigged and racist one. This belief explains differences in outcomes, including educational ones, based on cultural differences between groups, thus avoiding the allegation that this explanation is 'racist'. From this perspective, 'racism' requires explaining differences based on biological differences, not cultural ones. Colour-blind racism also suggests that any attempt to redress this long history of racial injustice through education, the law, or any other means is considered racist because it would mean that groups are not being treated equally. As a racial ideology, colour-blind racism provides a way of thinking that assures those in racially dominant positions that any educational advantages they have received in this global higher education system are not the result of racial power, but a fair and legitimate process. While this racial ideology has been most often developed to explain the reproduction of racist social orders in Western contexts such as the US, there are similar phenomena in non-Western societies such as 'caste-blindness' in India (see Rathod 2022).

Another related concept that explains the relationship between cognition and the reproduction of the racial status quo is *racial grammar*. Eduardo Bonilla-Silva (2012) frames racial grammar as a 'distillate' of racial ideology (174). Racial grammars are formed through racial ideology and become inscribed in the vocabularies we use day in and day out.

Racial grammars help reproduce the uneven patterns of a racialised social system through 'shaping the significant ways we see or don't see race in social phenomena, how we frame matters as racial or not race-related, even how we feel about race matters' (Bonilla-Silva 2012, 174). Bonilla-Silva offers an example from American education to explain how racial grammar both universalises Whiteness and establishes Whiteness as an unspoken and unseen social norm against which other ways of life are indexed and measured. In the US, there are colleges and universities and then there are Historically Black Colleges and Universities (HBCUs). The former institutions are those where Whiteness is unnamed and assumed, whereas the latter have '(t)he 'racial character ... tattooed in their very name' (Bonilla-Silva 2012, 183). This racial grammar establishes the notion that all American colleges and universities should be assumed to be White, and not Black. This automatic assumption, of course, is rooted in a long history that has constructed the superiority and centrality of Whiteness through associations with intelligence and advancement. By contrast, colleges and universities that are deemed to be not White because of their history, composition, or orientation must be identified as Historically Black. Like racial ideology, racial grammar constructs a cognitive map that burnishes the reputation of White colleges and universities through positioning Black colleges and universities as neither universal nor of the same standard. In this way, a racial grammar 'helps reproduce the racial order as just the way things are' (Bonilla-Silva 2012, 174). Given the danger posed by both racial grammar and ideology, Bonilla-Silva (2012) calls for an 'epistemology of racial emancipation' that challenges and provides an alternative to the universalisation and invisibilisation of Whiteness (187).

These cognitive concepts such as racial ideology and racial grammar can be criticised for the passive ways in which they construct those within positions of domination and subordination. With the concept of racial ideology, for example, it can seem to rest on a rendition of human nature in which people are passively lulled into some kind of stupor, of not being able to see the world as it really is, that makes them unknowingly contribute to the racial status quo. With racial grammar, it can seem as if people are parroting a vocabulary without even knowing it. As a result, some critical scholars prefer concepts that point to the active rather than passive ways in which people learn to think or not think, see or not see, feel or not feel about race matters. One example in the repertoire of concepts that reckon with the racial politics of cognition is *racial ignorance* (Mueller 2020).

Racial ignorance explains how racial groups *actively* approach knowledge to conserve and protect their material interests within a racially structured society (Mueller 2020). A key figure in this school of thought is Charles Mills (2007). Racial ignorance draws attention to the active ways in which individuals and educational institutions ignore knowledge that might challenge the racial status quo. The focus on an active process of ignoring knowledge to protect racial interests rather than passive mystification by knowledge marks the difference between racial ignorance and racial ideology. Racial ignorance therefore does not use terms such as 'obscuring', 'hiding', or 'concealing'. Such notions are associated with the *hidden curriculum* (Anyon 1980), which refers to how people learn norms, beliefs, and practices that reproduce their position in society without being overtly taught them. By contrast, racial ignorance points towards how, for example, individuals and institutions actively erase knowledge, say, through what we might call a *race-avoidant curriculum*, not a hidden curriculum. A race-avoidant curriculum is a curriculum that does not teach how histories of 'race' and racism have shaped the present world.

Racial ideology and racial ignorance, however, are not the only useful concepts to think about the significant relationship between knowledge, cognition, and racial power. Post-colonial and decolonial thought has also contributed concepts that engage with the politics of knowledge and cognition. However, these concepts tend to focus more on the violent outcomes of knowledge politics, outcomes that can be somewhat masked by terms such as racial ideology, racial grammar, and racial ignorance. For example, the post-colonial concept of *epistemic violence* refers to the ways in which the knowledge systems of colonially subjugated groups are silenced, dismissed, and devalued, if not destroyed (Spivak 1988, 280). Epistemic violence is always intimately intertwined with direct and physical violence against those who are deemed to possess knowledge that does not matter or are deemed to have limited rational capacity to produce knowledge that matters. In this way, epistemic violence is intimately tied to processes of racialisation whereby subjugated individuals within systems of colonial power are deemed to be incapable of producing thoughts that rise to the level of knowledge produced by those positioned as European and White because they are inferior or primitive, or both. In this way, epistemic violence is a way of discrediting subjugated people's capacity to speak the truth of their social existence. Given that these truths challenge systems of racial and colonial domination, epistemic violence is one way in which the historical legacies of colonialism can endure in the present.

Decolonial thought, particularly from Latin American contexts, has introduced concepts that are related to, but distinct from, this post-colonial concept of epistemic violence. Preferred terms within this school of thought end with the suffix '-*icide*', thus denoting murder and killing. Key decolonial concepts of *epistemicide, spiritualicide,* and *scholasticide* point to an inextricable relationship to *genocide* in the modern/colonial world (see Grosfoguel 2013). Epistemicide refers to the act of killing knowledge and knowledge systems. Epistemicide has historically occurred through destroying repositories of knowledge, such as burning books or libraries that belong to a particular group of subjugated people within a colonial system of power and domination. It can also occur through killing elders in Indigenous communities where knowledge is passed through oral traditions. Spiritualicide refers to the destruction of spirituality. Secularism has positioned religion and spirituality as irrelevant to the political arena where reason should prevail. Secularism is a fundamental principle of the Western world where Christianity is seen as compatible with secular forms of political governance, unlike, say, Islam. For this reason, spiritualicide has happened historically in the modern/colonial world through forced or coerced conversion. Finally, scholasticide refers to 'the arrest, detention or killing of teachers, students and staff, and the destruction of educational infrastructure' (United Nations Human Rights Office of the High Commissioner 2024). This concept was first introduced by Oxford-based Palestinian scholar, Karma Nabulsi, in her analysis of the destruction of educational infrastructure in Palestine. From this vantage point, those who kill knowledge systems and educational infrastructure for disseminating knowledge also kill the people who produce and use them. The killing of teachers and students, and demolishing educational infrastructure, destroys the relay of knowledge from one generation to the next.

While each of these concepts—epistemicide, spritualicide, and scholasticide—are different, they each illustrate how education is implicated in the elimination of ways of knowing and ways of being, if not the killing of people. Racialised populations can be constructed as if they do not and cannot produce or disseminate knowledge in ways that are fit for modernity. They can be either positioned as people who are ineducable or people with stunted educability. As a result, they are positioned as a different kind of human, a human that lacks the same capacity for reason as the modern subject, and therefore can become the legitimate targets of forced assimilation through education and extreme violence, including genocide.

It is not necessary to decide about which of these concepts—racial ideology, racial ignorance, epistemic violence, epistemicide, scholasticide, and genocide—is better in explaining how education contributes to the reproduction of the global system of White domination. It may be beneficial to combine them to establish transnational linkages whereby multiple phenomena, operating in different ways, maintain and sustain this global system of racialised domination. For example, consider how teaching Palestinian history in US educational contexts interlinks with the genocide in occupied Gaza. Bill Bigelow (2024) has argued that US school curriculum supports the genocide in Palestine. He has reviewed popular World History textbooks taught in American schools, including *Glencoe's World History* (2005) and *Modern World History* (1999). The former textbook begins its history of Palestine with Jewish immigration between the two world wars. It does not acknowledge the history of Muslim people in Palestine prior to that point. The latter textbook also frames the failure of Palestinian statehood on Palestinian people who refused to accept the partition of Israel in 1948. From a racial ideological perspective, these textbooks naturalise and legitimise Israeli occupation of Palestinian territories, as well as the expulsion and killing of its people, through concealing knowledge. However, some might point out that this analytical approach, one that draws on the concepts of racial ideology and hidden curriculum, obscures the fact that educators, students, and textbook authors are actively ignoring the history of Palestine and the Palestinian people. For this reason, the concept of racial ignorance may be more applicable. Further still, the denial of Palestinian voices and perspectives within a curriculum may be seen as an act of epistemic violence, suggesting that Palestinian people are incapable of knowing or speaking to the truth and reality of their conditions. And yet, racial ideology, racial ignorance, and epistemic violence do not capture what is occurring with respect to attacks on educational infrastructure in Palestine. In Palestine, schools, universities, and libraries are being destroyed (scholasticide) and this historical phenomenon is tied to a centuries long history of Western colonial projects destroying Muslim repositories of knowledge (epistemicide) (see Grosfoguel 2013). Both the killing of Palestinian knowledge and the killing of Palestinian people are rooted in fundamental belief within a global racial order that positions the Muslim subject as outside the frame of Western modern rationality and is therefore killable.

It is therefore neither necessary nor beneficial to believe that one suite of concepts from one perspective is better than the other in explaining the reproduction of this world-system. The important point is to establish transnational linkages across this global system of White domination. Establishing these linkages requires using multiple concepts that are fit for different contexts. In this example, it was too necessary to show how racial ideology or ignorance in the US context has been linked to epistemicide, scholasticide, and genocide in the Palestinian context. After all, it is impossible to imagine that this genocide would be taking place without broad American electoral support. The two are related but require concepts from different theoretical perspectives. When combined, they point to the critical, simultaneous, and transnational work that needs to be done. Combating racial ignorance in one context and stopping the destruction of schools and universities, and the murdering and starvation of teachers and students, in another are both necessary. Stopping one depends upon stopping the other. This example thus illustrates how employing concepts from different traditions allows for making transnational linkages that guide us towards multi-sited strategies for global critical action against elimination in the modern/colonial world-system.

Emotions

What people know and how they feel about what they know, and how people know and how they feel as they know, are fundamental aspects of learning. In education, the overwhelming tendency is to approach feelings as private and individual concerns, not social and political ones. However, sociological perspectives hold the view that emotions *are* social and political concerns. Emotions play a key role in forging social groups that struggle to maintain or contest societies structured in dominance. Today, for example, White people's sense of material and symbolic loss of power in Western liberal democracies is fuelling political movements that capitalise on this White rage, resentment, and grievance (see Hooker 2017). These are examples of *racialised emotions*, a key concept in sociological accounts of structural racism (Bonilla-Silva 2019). Racialised emotions are the 'socially engendered emotions in racialised societies' (Bonilla-Silva 2019, 3). This concept assumes that both positive and negative emotions—fear, pride, disgust, anger, joy, happiness, love, contempt, guilt, embarrassment, shame—are fundamental social forces in, as Bonilla-Silva (2019) puts it, 'shaping the house of racism' (2). From this perspective, emotions help forge groups based on 'race' that have a collective interest in either preserving or maintaining the uneven distribution of material and symbolic rewards within a racialised social system. It is necessary to focus attention on how the circulation of feelings around the world, as well as the racialisation of people through emotions, contributes to the reproduction of a global racial order. This perspective is needed to account, for example, how Islamophobia, literally 'the fear of Islam', shapes educational systems and practices throughout the world. This perspective must explain how various emotions maintain a global system of White dominance and propose how emotions might be learned differently to imagine and create alternatives to it.

The dominant approach to emotions in educational scholarship and practice in the West is shaped by liberalism. The view that education in the West should be concerned with cognition and knowledge, and not emotions and feelings, is itself a historical product of *political liberalism*. Political liberalism does not refer to left-leaning politics. Rather, political liberalism is concerned with promoting individual liberty. To provide this liberty, liberal democracies must establish a civil society that is governed by reason, not passion. From this standpoint, education must focus on cognition and knowledge, not feelings and emotions, to develop children and young people's capacity for reason. This capacity for reason includes preventing emotions from interfering with being rational. This capacity for reason is also deeply tied to political liberalism's belief in *tolerance* in liberal democratic societies. Tolerance means the capacity to manage one's disapproval for categories of people, their beliefs, and their customs. To become tolerant, one must learn to manage feelings of *intolerance*, such as fear, anger, and disgust towards others. In this way, teaching people to manage their emotions is seen as central to the development of tolerant individuals who can bear political rights and responsibilities in liberal democracy (see Drerup 2018).

While political liberalism has shaped how Western educational systems and institutions approach emotions, *economic liberalism* has also been a major influence. Economic liberalism is concerned with forging a market economy based on individualism. In economically liberal societies, education must prepare students with the skills and knowledge to have an equal opportunity to participate in this market economy. Historically, emotions have not been considered an important aspect of this education. However, since the 1990s, there has been a greater appreciation for the role of emotions in making people more effective workers, particularly in a service-based economy. In such an economy, interacting with others, and being sensitive to different people's concerns and needs, is now a labour prerequisite. From this perspective, emotions are to be harnessed for the benefit of being a more productive worker who can contribute more effectively to a market economy and experience economic success. This shift has influenced dominant educational thought and practice in Western contexts. Emotions have been increasingly valued for fostering academic achievement and cultivating human capital (see Heckman and Kautz 2012). Through *social and emotional learning*, teachers are expected to employ strategies that help children and young people learn how to understand, manage, and express their emotions.

Through this liberal approach to emotions, the politics of emotions are too easily ignored. But the politics of emotions are central to the role education plays in reproducing the racial status quo. For example, arguments against teaching the history of transatlantic slavery in the US have often focused on protecting White children from feeling guilt, shame, or hatred for themselves or their nations. These 'chilling affects', as Woody Holton (2024, 199) aptly terms them, suppress the teaching histories of US racial violence. Through producing not only racial ignorance, but also preserving feelings of innocence, this race-avoidant curriculum maintains the legitimacy of Whiteness as the dominant structural position within American society. After all, Whiteness is meant to stand for civilisation (and liberalism) not barbarism (and illiberalism). This example shows how emotions are contested for the role they might play in the educational reproduction of societies structured in racial dominance.

Critics of US education from the political left have also criticised social and emotional learning for the role it plays in targeting racially inferiorised children and young people for engaging in behaviour that does not conform to White middle-class norms (see Dalrymple and Phillips 2024). In this sense, social and emotional learning is framed as an institutional mechanism of *cultural racism*. Racially inferiorised children are viewed as lacking the capacity to manage their emotions, and this lack stems from their social upbringing. As a result, the blame for any negative life outcomes they experience, particularly economic ones, can be attributed to a cultural deficiency, not a lack of opportunity. The assertion that racially inferiorised children and young people have a diminished or deficient capacity to manage their emotions protects and preserves the racial status quo. Indeed, scholars in Black studies, for example, have observed how the racialisation of Black people arises through, in part, constructing them beholden to animalistic impulses because they lack the capacity for reason (see Freeburg 2017). Through a relational process of racialisation, White people are constructed as those with an *interiority,* the inner nature of their being, that allows them to manage their animalistic impulses so that they can participate in a liberal democratic order. In this way, paying attention to both racialised emotions and what we might call *emotional racialisation,* or racialisation through one's ascribed relative capacity to manage emotions, is critical. Accounting for both elements is necessary to establish transnational linkages that explain how educational systems maintain and sustain this global system of White domination.

The importance of this perspective can be seen in examining the contested role of emotions in teaching the history of transatlantic slavery, not only in the US, but in other national contexts. As we have stated, there have been considerable debates about teaching the history of transatlantic slavery in the US, particularly after the introduction of *The 1619 Project,* by Nikole Hannah-Jones. This public scholarship sought to address political silences and omissions in the official history of the US. This project sought to show how every aspect of the nation that followed was shaped by the introduction of slavery to the Virginia colony in the early seventeenth century, more than 150 years before the nation was founded. After this project was introduced in 2021, parents, often White people, organised in local school districts to combat the teaching of this project in schools. They argued that it produces feelings of guilt, shame, and hatred in White children about themselves and the nation. In other words, they argued that schools were not treating White children equally through teaching this history because White children's feelings would be hurt in ways that non-White children would not experience. Through this line of argument, the teaching of this history is suppressed in ways that protect the innocence and ignorance associated with this structural position of Whiteness. A racialised social system is reproduced through this innocence and ignorance because these feelings enable those in the dominant position to believe that the rewards that they enjoy in life have been earned fairly. A fair social system does not need to be changed. Of course, this focus on White feelings also ignores how such a curriculum might affect Black children. In this way, their feelings are overlooked as if they do not exist. This oversight sustains the anti-Black idea that Black people themselves, in this case, children and young people in schools, do not have an interiority that matters. This example is an illustration of how a racialised social system is sustained through both racialised emotions and emotional racialisation. In other words, this system perpetuates anti-Blackness through protecting White people from guilt and shame, while racialising Black people as those who do not have the capacity for emotions that matter.

Making transnational linkages in educational phenomena is crucial to this global critical race perspective. It is important to recognise, for example, that political silences and omissions about the history of transatlantic slavery also exist in the history curriculum of other key nodes in the transatlantic slave trade, including West African schools. And yet, there are few White people—teachers or students—in West African educational contexts. Nonetheless, in Ghana, Afua Hirsch, has noted that textbooks, such as *Basic Social Studies for Junior High Schools,* do not mention the brutal realities of slavery. This account of education in Ghana resonated with Deborah Yeboah, an artist, art teacher, and education scholar from Ghana. Yeboah (2024) has argued that emotions are key to the silencing of this history in Ghana because this history is so painful, if not traumatising, for Ghanaians to remember. There is a risk that teaching slavery in Ghana will lead students to see their nation, Africanness, and Blackness as defined by pain, suffering, and historical trauma. However, she calls for a curriculum that recognises that this history of slavery still wounds Black people today through anti-Black racism and violence. As a result, there is still a need for healing that reckons with this painful history and its historical continuity. She therefore calls for an art curriculum that engages children and young people with the 'Door of No Return', the infamous threshold through which Black African people were stripped of their humanity. She calls for a curriculum that interrogates this threshold as both a space of nightmares and a space for imaginative potential (Yeboah 2024, 141).

The above example thus shows the importance of making transnational linkages in education through racialised emotions and emotional racialisation. Together, these processes work simultaneously to contribute to the reproduction of a world that is fundamentally anti-Black. This anti-Blackness is produced through not only producing epistemic silences in the curriculum but through protecting the emotions of those who benefit from an anti-Black world. Moreover, this anti-Back world is produced through perpetuating the idea that Black people do not have an interiority that either matters or is as emotionally mature as other racialised groups. This construction of Black being (or non-being) poses an existential and global threat to Black people.

The concepts examined above provide a variety of tools that can explain how educational systems and practices are implicated in maintaining and sustaining a global system of White domination. This explanation is necessary because the racial orders that we have inherited are not merely intra-national in nature. They are, and have been since the long sixteenth century, if not earlier, international in nature. Educational systems and practices are thus implicated in not only contributing to racist outcomes 'at home' but also racist outcomes 'abroad'. These outcomes can be highly variable, yet still interconnected, across these various contexts. However, it is necessary to recognise that routine forms of extreme violence are not aberrations, or exceptions, to this long history of the modern/colonial world. They are endemic to it. As a result, how knowledge and feelings, ways of knowing and feeling, are learned in different contexts in ways that enable this violence to occur with relative impunity is an important area of theoretical concern.

CHAPTER 4

Applying a Global Critical Race Theory of Education

Abstract Since 9/11, the Global War on Terror has revitalised a long-standing, global racial, and colonial ideology that positions Muslimness as a threat to civility, rationality, and progress. The Global War on Terror has remade educational systems throughout the world by asking institutions and educators to prevent extremism and terrorism. The adoption of a global 'countering violent extremism' (CVE) agenda has been one of the principle mechanisms by which Muslim people, and people mistaken as Muslim, are racialised as a threat to be surveilled, managed, and even eliminated within modern nation-states across the world. As a result, education has become a site through which racialized knowledge and emotions about Muslimness is produced and circulated, which in turn re-inscribes the putative racial threat the Muslim populations are thought to pose to modernity. In this chapter, we illustrate the power of a global critical race theory of education to explain and contest the circulation of anti-Muslim racism in educational contexts throughout the world.

Keywords Social theories · Educational Theories · Global Approach · Critical Race Theory · Race · Racism · Decolonization · Islamophobia

© The Author(s) 2026   79
T. Denmead and A. Shareef, *Rethinking Critical Race Theory*, Palgrave
Studies in Race, Inequality and Social Justice in Education,
https://doi.org/10.1007/978-3-032-07749-3_4

Throughout this book, we have introduced an array of concepts that we think are useful in beginning to explain how educational systems and practices throughout the world might maintain and sustain a global system of White domination. This explanation is necessary to challenge any complacency towards the racially violent social realities that we inhabit. This explanation is necessary to understand the interconnectedness of racial violence throughout the world. Through these concepts, this global critical race perspective orients scholars, students, and activists towards making transnational linkages in education that develop our understanding of how education contributes to the reproduction and contestation of a global system of 'race' and racism. While we have focused considerably so far on tools to think with, we have not focused on the question of methodology. We do not intend to be prescriptive about methodology. There is a danger in assuming that if the correct methodology is chosen, then the knowledge produced will be more valid and legitimate. We do not hold this view. Instead, the challenge is not so much choosing a methodology, but thinking critically about the assumptions that are framing the choice of, and expectations for one.

Critical race theory has always been deeply suspicious of positivist orientations to knowledge production. The demand for facts and data, or evidence of statistically significant causal relations, is often used as a strategy to minimise the effects of 'race' and racism. If statistical significance cannot be observed, racism does not exist! Moreover, positivism assumes that there is a neutral, objective, and transparent way of producing knowledge about 'race' and racism. However, positivistic methods often are employed to study 'race' and racism based on the assumption that racism must be intended by an individual and directed towards another individual towards whom they are racially prejudiced. That is not how critical race theory approaches racism.

Critical race theory has therefore tended to rely on counter-storytelling as a method to challenge the apparent naturalness of racial ideologies—such as colour-blindness, colourism, biological racism, Islamophobia. Counter-storytelling is addressed from the standpoint of those who can bear witness to the falseness of these ideologies. Counter-storytelling often involves some kind of testimonial that counters the epistemic violence that is endemic to any racialised social system. Counter-storytelling can be questioned for the extent to which it provides social explanations for how such systems are maintained and sustained. Nonetheless, there are countless examples of scholars and activists who have used counter-storytelling to do so. bell hooks is perhaps one of the most effective critical race and feminist scholars who used counter-storytelling. For example, hooks (1992) used the method to call attention to the ways in which, for example, desire is continuously exploited in a manner that maintains and sustains the racial status quo.

That said, it is necessary for any methodological choice to be oriented towards how 'race' and racism is interconnected across contexts, how 'race' and racism draws downward from racial ideologies and feelings that are circulating globally, and how 'race' and racism at the local level contributes to that global circulation of racial ideologies and feelings. In this sense, any study that draws on this theoretical orientation, and contributes to the further development of this orientation, must be attuned to both the interconnectedness of multiple contexts and the multi-scalar nature of 'race' and racism.

From this vantage point, qualitative methodologies that attend to multiple contexts simultaneously, such as multi-sited ethnography or case study, are an obvious choice. New methods might emerge, such as *transnational counter-storytelling*, that amplify the voices of those who have crossed borders and experienced local educational manifestations of this global system of 'race' and racism in transnational ways. There have also been recent pushes to use quantitative methods in critical race theory while, at the same time, refuting its claims of objectivity and neutrality (Gillborn et al. 2023). It is conceivable that scholars and students attempt to make transnational linkages through the critical use of quantitative methods. This perspective is also concerned with animating the imagination and activating the production of worlds that cut against the grain of this system of White domination. In this way, arts-based methodologies may be particularly suitable. Whatever the choice may be, we caution against the assumption that the choice of one methodology over another will produce outcomes that are more or less legitimate or valid. The more important challenge is how to think with concepts that provide a social explanation of how education contributes to the reproduction of this global system of White imagination, and, in turn, create new vocabularies that both provide new explanations and provoke the sociological imagination.

Below we provide a case study to provide an illustration of how to think with this global perspective. This case study focuses on the global practice of counter violent extremism in education. This example provides a useful illustration for several reasons. First, this case study shows how to establish the interconnectedness of educational phenomena in reproducing a global racial system rather than merely comparing phenomena across their specific contexts. Second, this case study allows us to show the need to engage in an analysis on multiple scales to establish both the historical continuity of this global system and the historical shifts that occur at individual, group, and national levels. Third, this case study allows us to show how education systems draw down from a global project—the Global War on Terror—to sustain this global system through education. In this case, education becomes a mechanism through which nation-states as a modern/colonial racial apparatus attempt to move away from Muslimness to strengthen their position within this global matrix of racial power. Through explaining the interconnectedness of this system, people can begin to develop an understanding of the need for imagining and creating worlds that are not predicated on racialised elimination.

Case Study: The Global Rise of Counter-Violent Extremism in Education Following the attacks on the World Trade Center on 11 September 2001, the US and a coalition of allies launched a global military campaign against terrorism known as the Global War on Terror. The Global War on Terror began with military invasions and operations in Afghanistan (2001–2021) and Iraq (2003–2011). In its second phase, which is still ongoing as we write, the Global War on Terror has focused on pre-empting terrorism throughout the world, not simply pursuing and punishing perpetrators after a terrorist event has occurred (Kundnani 2014). As we will see, this focus on pre-empting terrorism has had a profound impact on education and those positioned and racialised as Muslim subjects throughout the world.

Since its inception, the Global War on Terror has been criticised for how it defines terrorism. After all, terrorism is only a tactic. Terrorism employs violence against non-combatants to achieve political or ideological aims. The Global War on Terror thus proposes a war against a tactic rather than, say, a nation-state. Critics have pointed out that the US and its allies have also used terror, or state terrorism, in waging this global campaign, particularly using torture, sexual humiliation, and drones. This fact reflects one of the key aspects of the nation-state form—it positions itself as the arbiter of what is deemed to be legitimate political violence and illegitimate political violence based on whether such violence serves or opposes its interests (see Reddy 2011). This ambiguity around the legitimacy of political violence in the Global War on Terror has led critics to suggest that this war is in fact 'a war against Muslim opponents of the West, if not Islam itself' (see Katz 2010). It is important to recognise, as we have argued earlier in this book, that the racialised category of Muslimness is both expansive and elastic. It can include people who are not Muslim but are targeted as if they are Muslim.

This Global War on Terror matters to educationists because it deploys efforts to regulate Muslim populations in efforts to prevent terrorism and these efforts to regulate Muslim populations have circulated globally. These regulatory measures that have featured in the Global War on Terror have been far less recognised than military campaigns in countries such as Afghanistan and Iraq. Nonetheless, strategies such as public diplomacy, cultural exchange, economic development, community engagement, and the promotion of education and human rights have been central to these counterinsurgency efforts. These pre-emptive strategies are of particular interest to educationists because education is often positioned as the primary strategy that can prevent people from turning to terrorism. However, if the Global War on Terror is understood as a war against Muslim opponents of the West, if not Islam itself, then counterinsurgency through education risks becoming a tool that perpetuates the notion that the Muslimness itself is a threat to a global order defined by the West. There are multiple reasons why Muslimness may be deemed to pose a threat to this global system of White domination, from the Orientalist associations with barbarity and primitiveness that are thought to be the root cause of terrorism (not anti-Western, anti-colonial political sentiment) (Said 1978), to the perceived threat that Muslims are more loyal to a global community of Muslims ('ummah') than they are any individual nation-state (Sayyid 2014). Critical scholars must therefore attend to how the Global War on Terror circulates anti-Muslim ideas, beliefs, and practices throughout the world.

Critical race theory of education has paid little attention to the Global War on Terror. There are, of course, multiple reasons for this trend. First and foremost, as Damian Breen (2018) puts it, 'applying a theory of 'race' to look at issues around religion might seem at best restrictive and at worst problematic' (31). Applying 'race' to religion can seem problematic because people of the same religious faith can have different racial identities. A White Muslim, for example, might not experience overt racism or be disadvantaged by their religious identity during their lives in the same way as a non-White Muslim. Applying 'race' to religion risks disregarding the nuances of how Muslims do and do not experience 'race' and racism throughout the world. As a result, there is still a dominant tendency to view 'race' in terms of 'colour' and religion in terms of ethnicity, or culture. This distinction, however, can fail to explain how people are racialised—or deemed to be a different kind of human, an inferior kind of human, or a historically immature, or primitive, kind of human—through their ascribed Muslimness.

Our perspective challenges the view that thinking about 'race' in terms of culture is fundamentally a new phenomenon, a tendency that is reinforced through calling racism based on cultural differences 'neo-racism' (Balibar 1991, 21). The fact of the matter is that cultural racism is as old as the formation of a crusading society against Muslims and Jews even if the term 'race' was not necessarily used. Cultural racism therefore has a very long history, one that has been far more prevalent and dominant historically speaking than that of biological racism. From this vantage point, religion is a marker of cultural difference, and anti-Muslim racism is characterised by a belief in the view that Islam is incompatible with Western life-styles and traditions, and perhaps, upon closer inspection, by a belief that Muslim people are inferior and pose a threat to the Western-defined system of White domination. Now, for nearly three decades, The Global War on Terror has contributed to maintaining and sustaining a world-system that is structured through a long historical construction of Islam and Muslims (and Muslim-adjacent people) as inferior, immature, and incompatible with the modern world. Throughout the Global War on Terror, we have seen this longstanding modern/colonial desire to eliminate Muslim populations, evidenced by the estimate of over 430,000 civilians (and then 940,000 people overall) who were killed by direct post-9/11 war violence in Iraq, Afghanistan, Syria, Yemen, and Pakistan between 2001 and 2023 (Watson Institute for International and Public Affairs 2023), as well as the nearly 60,000 people killed in occupied Gaza during the war since the Hamas attacks on 7 October 2023.

With this long historical understanding, a global critical theory perspective of education points to the process of transnational racialisation through religion. Transnational racialisation refers to the global racial presumptions and practices that interact with national and local racial projects to reproduce hegemonic understandings of Whiteness (Christian 2019, 181). The Global War on Terror, we contend, has contributed to processes of transnational racialisation. It has produced racial presumptions and practices about Muslim subjectivities and Islam itself. Muslims and Muslim-adjacent people, particularly those from Middle Eastern and African nations, have been constructed as individuals who are not fit for Western liberal democracies because they lack the capacity for reason and tolerance. The source of this incapacity is not biological, but religious and cultural. This racialisation of Muslim subjectivities through the Global War on Terror then interacts with national and local racial projects to reproduce hegemonic understandings of Whiteness. For example, Whiteness can be constructed at local and national levels as a structural position that signifies tolerance, civilisation, intelligence, and benevolence in relation to its presumed lack, Muslimness. We see this process arise, for example, in right-wing political movements that have mobilised around the very notion that Western nations need stronger borders to protect themselves not from terrorism per se, but from an influx of Muslims who are deemed to be incompatible with Western, White, and Judeo-Christian life-styles and traditions.

Countering violent extremism (CVE) provides one case study for educationists to consider as a mechanism that sustains this centuries-old world-system of White domination through the racialisation of Muslim subjectivities. President Obama launched this strategy at a CVE Summit in Washington in 2015 and during the September 2015 session at the UN General Assembly. CVE, both as a field and set of practices, is oriented towards disrupting the ideological, economic, and political conditions that are believed to radicalise individuals to commit acts of violence. Its aims are to 'reduce specific political or social and economic factors that contribute to community support for violent extremism in identifiable areas or put particular segments of populations at high risk of violent extremist radicalisation and recruitment to violence' (The United States Department of State and USAID 2016, 6). Today, CVE is promoted by a range of powerful national and global institutions including the U.S. Bureau of Counterterrorism and Countering Violent Extremism, the United Nations Counter-Terrorism Committee (CTC), the United Nations Global Counter-Terrorism Coordination Compact, the United Nations Office of Counter-Terrorism (UNOCT), and United Nations Educational, Scientific and Cultural Organisation (UNESCO).

Through the global reach of these institutions, some version of CVE policy is found in almost every country on this planet. There is the 'Plan National de Prévention de la Radicalisation' in France; the 'Living

Safe Together Initiative' in Australia; the 'National Strategy to Counter Violent Extremism' in Kenya; the 'National Strategy on Countering Radicalization to Violence' in Canada; the 'National Program for Tolerance' in Abu Dhabi/United Arab Emirates; the 'National Plan for Citizen Security and Social Peace' in Costa Rica; and, the 'Preventing and Countering Violent Extremism' plan in Bangladesh. These policies employ a range of techniques including counter-extremist messaging, surveillance, policing, capacity building, economic empowerment, civil society promotion, and undermining terrorist ideology. UNESCO has identified education as a key tool in this global CVE strategy. It has assisted United Nations (UN) member states in implementing CVE policies and practices in educational contexts (United Nations Human Rights Office of the High Commissioner 2023). This agenda is delivered through the Global Citizenship Education framework. Through this framework, UNESCO works with national educational systems to build and strengthen their capacity to prevent violence extremism through education at all levels.

The global countering violent extremism (CVE) agenda emerges from a long history of colonialism that produced knowledge about racial and colonial difference. CVE initiatives, which claim to disrupt the ideological, economic, and political conditions believed to radicalise individuals into committing acts of violence, are rooted in tactics derived from military counterinsurgency doctrine. Historically, counterinsurgency knowledge was developed to suppress anti-colonial guerrilla movements seeking liberation from the British Empire in colonies such as India, Malaya, Kenya, Cyprus, and Northern Ireland during the late nineteenth and early to mid-twentieth centuries (Sabir 2017). These colonial-era techniques—involving community development, financial inducements, community policing for intelligence gathering and surveillance, and the dissemination of strategic communication (propaganda)—closely resemble the CVE strategies deployed globally today (Mesok 2022; Sabir 2017; Kundnani 2014). As Elizabeth Mesok (2025) explains, CVE functions as a form of counterinsurgency by blending violence with social engagement to maintain control over populations and eliminate those perceived as threats to the liberal international order. Crucially, the 'racial logic of colonial control found in British imperial policing is similarly present in current manifestations and policing of the 'violent extremist' or otherwise 'suspect' individual' (Mesok and Schildknecht 2025, 4). Viewed through this lens, CVE must be seen as reinforcing and sustaining a racialised social system that perpetuates colonial power relations, reinforcing the divide between those who are deemed to be worthy of state protection from violence and those who are deemed to be targets of state regulation, surveillance, and potentially physical violence. A global critical race theory perspective of education is therefore essential for exposing the enduring colonial legacy that shapes countering violent extremism.

Through a global critical perspective, we approach 'countering violent extremism' as a *global racial grammar*. That is, countering violent extremism does particular work in various contexts throughout the world to make Muslimness as a racialised category visible and invisible. Racial grammars serve to 'universalize and invisibilize Whiteness as an implicit social norm' against which other racialised groups are measured. In this case, 'countering violent extremism' as a racial grammar conjures the figure of the Muslim as a violent extremist, or as predisposed to violent extremism in relation to the figure of the White secularised Christian European who is posited as a rational actor predisposed to tolerance (Meghji 2021, 355). The determining factor in this relational formula is 'race'. As such, countering violent extremism as a global racial grammar seeks to maintain and sustain the dominant position of Whiteness with a global racial order. This global racial grammar operates through various terms in educational policy and practice such as safeguarding, extremism, terrorism, radicalisation, and global citizenship.

Consider the term radicalisation. Radicalisation has come to refer to the theological and socio-psychological conditions that lead an individual to identify with violent extremist ideology and take a trajectory towards committing an act of terrorism (Kundnani 2014). Some indicators of an individual's journey towards violence are an 'existential and spiritual search for identity', 'distortion and misuse of beliefs', and 'identification with collective grievances' (*Preventing Violent Extremism through Education: A Guide for Policy-Makers* 2017, 21). Crucially, radicalisation is a term that exclusively refers to political ideologies known as extremism and political violence known as terrorism. Extremism conjures a range of ideologies that have putative origins in 'radical Islam', such as Islamism, ideologies of jihad, calls for the restoration of a caliphate, and the rejection of Western imperialism in nations understood to be Muslim-dominant (Kundnani 2014). Terrorism conjures political violence committed by Muslim actors holding 'extremist views', which may be political views that are oppositional to Western imperialist projects (Corbin 2017). While in no way are we condoning political violence, racial grammars resist and diminish efforts to historicise and contextualise, but not defend, political violence. As a result, the racial grammar of radicalisation makes the Muslim figure visible as an ahistorical extremist, as someone who is just naturally predisposed to violence, without explicitly referring to the category of the Muslim. This racial grammar provides an organisational map for how people should understand and experience their social reality, and in turn, guides their actions to either maintain or contest this racial order. Muslim political violence cannot be explained except for the fact that Muslimness is the problem and therefore Muslimness should be regulated, if not eliminated.

The ostensibly non-referential nature of the term extremism is critical to its power as a racial grammar. After all, in counter-violent extremism policies in education, the link between radicalisation and Muslims is not always made explicitly clear. For example, in a UNESCO guide to policy-makers on preventing violent extremism through education, as well as a Department of Education guide to schools on implementing the UK's counter extremism strategy, there is no mention of terms that link the policy to Islam and Muslims (Department for Education 2023; United Nations Human Rights Office of the High Commissioner 2023). However, in other policy documents, the link between radicalisation and extremist ideologies rooted in Islam and Islamist-based political movements is clearly stated (HM Government 2024). This ambiguity allows counter extremism policy to evade charges of anti-Muslim racism. For our analysis here, it makes the vocabulary radicalisation a racial grammar which makes Muslim simultaneously visible and invisible as a race.

In the context of schools, the racial grammar of radicalisation casts Muslim pupils as inherently 'at risk', framing their identity and belief systems as potential precursors to terrorism. The language of 'risk' renders Muslimness as a racialised category presumed to possess a biocultural predisposition towards political violence. This framing draws on a transnational process of racialising Muslim identities as violent due to their association with Islam. This framing occurs through a relation with Whiteness, which is deemed to have a biocultural predisposition towards peaceful political engagement, and, increasingly in the contemporary context of Israel/Palestine, through a relation with both Jewish and Christian political subjectivities that are deemed to be tolerant, rational, and civilised. Within this logic, pupils racialised as Muslim, who may or may not be Muslim, are deemed suspect. Similarly, criticism of Western foreign policy—such as the extraction of resources, forced displacement, or the ongoing violence in countries understood as Muslim—is read, not as political consciousness, but as vulnerability to terrorist recruitment (Kundnani 2014).

A global critical race perspective recognises that these racial grammars are not confined to national borders but operate through global circuits of power and meaning. Nationally racialised social systems are shaped not only from the ground up but also from the top down, drawing upon a global racial ideology and grammar that is adapted to fit specific local contexts. National policymakers are not passive recipients of these frameworks; rather, they actively reinterpret and implement them in ways that align with local political cultures, histories, and conceptions of national identity. For example, unlike France and the UK, Finland does not require schools to monitor students for signs of radicalisation. Instead, its CVE approach focuses on fostering inclusion and student wellbeing as a preventative strategy (Niemi et al. 2018). In the UK, the racial grammar of CVE is expressed through the discourse of safeguarding vulnerable children (Coppock and McGovern 2014), while in France it takes the form of defending *laïcité* and Republican values. This French framework enforces strict religious neutrality and has recently criminalised so-called Islamist separatism, constructing it as a threat to the secular state (Annovi 2023). These differing grammars are rooted in national imaginaries and political traditions, shaping how terrorism is racialised and rendered raceless within each context. Whether through the UK's promotion of 'Fundamental British Values', France's emphasis on Republicanism, or China's deployment of state ideology, the construction of national identity is central to the implementation of CVE across national contexts (see Newman and Zhang 2021 for discussion of CVE in Chinese context). Yet the modalities of this racial grammar vary widely. In China, for instance, the state employs mass internment and forced re-education camps aimed at the sinicisation of the Turkic Muslim population in Xinjiang whereas, in the UK, schools and teachers have been positioned as extensions of the state's surveillance apparatus. These examples illustrate how the global racial grammar of CVE is not simply replicated across nations but is localised in ways that reinforce existing power structures and racial logics, contributing to a global racialised order under the banners of countering terrorism and maintaining social cohesion.

A global critical race perspective on education reveals how national-level racial ideologies and racial grammars are not only domestically significant but also world-shaping. The CVE global agenda operates through a form of police power—a mode of governance that compels populations to 'participate in their own security and ensure their own governability', often through financial incentives to nations throughout the world through developmental aid (Mesok 2022, 720). Numerous scholars have identified a security-development nexus within CVE initiatives, where development and peacebuilding efforts are harnessed to advance security objectives (see, for example, N. Nguyen 2023). Dominant understandings of radicalisation tend to attribute political violence to conditions such as ineffective security forces, economic deprivation, or the lack of civil liberties, rather than to ongoing forms of Western imperialism and colonisation—such as the occupations of Iraq and Afghanistan, the genocide in Palestine, and the indefinite detention of Muslim (and Muslim-adjacent) individuals without charge. As a result, NGOs in the development sector often adopt approaches that aim to modulate individual psyches by modifying civil society and promoting so-called 'protective factors' like social cohesion, economic stability, and access to healthcare (N. Nguyen 2023, 401). These interventions shift attention away from structural and geopolitical violence, narrowing the political horizons of civil society. By tethering security objectives to development and peacebuilding, CVE takes away the independence of civil society, demanding compliance with global security goals (Mesok 2022, 3). In this way, CVE becomes a tool of statecraft, particularly in conflict zones, where nations are pressured to reshape civil society in the image of 'internationally acceptable forms of governance' (Mesok 2022, 3). CVE, then, extends the logic of coloniality, making it clear that each nation-state throughout the world needs to pass through various stages of development that bring it in closer proximity to Western and European nations. As Mark Neocleous (2011) observes, the Global War on Terror represents 'the violent fabrication of world order' (p. 156)—a project in which CVE plays a central role in constructing formerly colonised nations and currently occupied territories as historically immature and uncivilised. This global critical race perspective allows us to see how racial grammar of CVE is world-shaping through not only shaping the actions of racial actors within nations, but also through positioning nations with a global racial order. Together, CVE becomes an active force in maintaining and sustaining a system of White domination through and beyond education.

This global critical race perspective on education calls us to imagine and actively create alternative worlds—worlds grounded in justice, equity, and the dignity of all life. The example above illustrates the strength and transformative promise of such a framework. It underscores the urgent need to rethink education not as a neutral or benevolent institution, but as a site that often sustains global Whiteness as a structural position of dominance and control. Rather than perpetuating these inequities, education holds the radical potential to foster new social realities—ones in which the right of all beings to exist, to thrive, and to shape their futures is fully recognised and honoured. Through this lens, the analysis of counter-extremism policies in education reveals the deep entanglements between local and national forms of anti-Muslim racism and the broader, global architecture of the War on Terror. Educational analyses grounded in a global critical race framework seek to disrupt the transnational processes of racialisation that render Muslim life eliminable, Muslim lands expatriable, and Muslim resources endlessly extractable. This form of analysis offers more than critique—it is a call to reimagine education as a powerful space for decolonial possibility, where all human life is seen as sacred, worthy of protection, and central to building more just and life-affirming futures for all.

CHAPTER 5

Conclusion

Abstract As critical race theory is weaponised by right-wing political movements to foment White resentment over perceived economic and cultural loss, now may not seem like the right moment to point out the limitations of critical race theory of education. However, the exercise of racial power that we are witnessing around the world—depopulation, re-education, state-sanctioned communal violence, genocide—gives us no choice. Critical race theory scholars must continue to rethink this orientation to expand its explanatory and resistive power. It is with this project in mind that the authors of this book set out to re-orient critical race theory of education towards the global and account for the threat that anti-Muslim racism poses to populations living in interconnected geographies around the world such as Palestine, India, Myanmar, and China. Our account urges critical race scholars of education to explain how a world-system, one that is predicated on the elimination of populations that threaten Western notions of rationality and progress, is reproduced through educational systems throughout the world. It gives renewed hope and inspiration to educators throughout the world who are already, and often quietly, engaging transgressive teaching to dismantle the norms, beliefs, standards, and practices that maintain White domination on a global scale. Our book is the beginning of a new, globally-oriented, educational project that is committed to protecting the flourishing of all genres of humanity.

© The Author(s) 2026   93
T. Denmead and A. Shareef, *Rethinking Critical Race Theory*, Palgrave
Studies in Race, Inequality and Social Justice in Education,
https://doi.org/10.1007/978-3-032-07749-3_5

Keywords Social theories · Educational Theories · Global Approach · Critical Race Theory · Race · Racism · Decolonization

As we have written this book, a series of jarring events have challenged the dominant Western conception of the world since World War II. As we write, this *liberal international order* appears to be crumbing. The Trump administration has placed tariffs on US imports of foreign goods in ways that have reversed decades of policy grounded in economic liberalism. Political liberalism seems to be under threat, too, as far-right populist and authoritarian parties overtake more traditional conservative parties in Western states. These parties have been riding a tide of cultural and economic resentment towards this liberal international order for favouring global elites and the rising middle class in developing countries. The commitment to liberal internationalism has also appeared to wane as Western governments have wavered, if not broken its promise, in defence of one nation it had claimed as its own—Ukraine. The US also withdrew from the Paris Agreement that commits countries throughout the world to reduce greenhouse gas emissions. And, finally, liberal democratic governments have aided, abetted, actively armed, and offered cover to the genocidal aims of the Israeli settler colonial project that is forcing the Palestinian population to surrender their homeland through starvation, disease, displacement, and death. As we noted in the introduction, there are other political projects threatening Muslim life in various parts of the world—India, Myanmar, Kashmir, China—but these crises have failed to crystallise global attention.

These events only seem jarring and unprecedented when we ignore the longer global history of this Western racial order. From this perspective, the history of the Western world is one in which the nation-state as a racial and colonial political form emerged through the construction and ranking of human difference and was then exported to the rest of the world through a long history of colonisation and decolonisation. The nation-state is predicated on the notion that the population of the nation is bound together in racial and cultural terms, and those who do not conform to that dominant norm must be regulated, expelled, and banished to living conditions that are closer to dying than living, what Mbembe (2003, 40) called *death-worlds*. The racial-colonial form of the nation-state is also predicated on the claim that Western Europeans were the first to become enlightened enough and rational enough to bear the responsibility of political and economic self-governance. All other racialised peoples throughout the world were positioned on a temporal horizon as stuck in a state of nature, lingering in perpetual delay and underdevelopment, a positioning that legitimises the exercise of violence to bring them into modernity. In this way, the Western nation-state became the arbiter of violence against racialised and colonised populations within its borders and racialised and colonised populations beyond its borders. The violence of regulating, policing, colonising, and developing racialised and colonised populations both 'at home' and 'abroad' is considered rational, a necessary step in the development of humanity. Resistance to this violence is pathologised as the violence of the irrational, violence that is outside the violence of those who belong to the rules-based order. In the racial grammar that prevails today, this violence is most referred to as 'terrorism'. Taking the long history of the liberal international order, we point out that its violence and irrationality in the present are neither aberrations nor exceptions, but rather endemic. This violence and irrationality are perennial features that have been actively ignored by those who have benefited and continue to benefit from the modern/colonial world-system.

As we write, 'critical race theory' is being used as a political weapon to attack the autonomy of higher education institutions, defund scientific research, and detain and deport international students for their political views. The attack on 'critical race theory' is inextricably linked to the ongoing production of occupied Palestine as a death-world and the suppression of anti-genocide, anti-racist solidarity and protest. It is impossible to understand the attack on 'critical race theory' outside of this transnational context. For this very reason, we have found it urgent and necessary to critically and constructively rethink critical race theory and account for the global in the analysis of local and national forms of racism in education. In this book, we have argued that this rethinking is a necessary corrective to the starting points found in critical race theory that naturalises the American nation-state as a social and political form and isolates it from other nation-states. This orientation has provincialised critical race theory and limited its theoretical power to explaining 'race' and racism in US educational contexts, or even worse, exposed it to the criticism of perpetuating the idea that 'race' and racism is a problem specific to the US due primarily to its history of plantation slavery (with its history of settler colonialism overshadowed). It is precisely these reasons that have led to the dismissal of critical race theory of education within our experiences of teaching and studying in the UK. Nonetheless, we believe that critical race theory remains a useful framework to think with—or rather to rethink—precisely because it allows us to pay attention to the internal logics and processes of 'race' and racism at the national scale. Our contribution draws transnational connections between local and national racial projects and takes the making of the world-system as the originator of their racial logics (Meghji 2022).

Throughout this book, we have attempted to work towards a framework that urges education scholars to recognise that 'race' and racism shape interactions between actors in educational contexts, between educational systems and practices with a national context, and between nation-states and international actors in a global context. Individuals, educational institutions, and national education systems can attempt to occupy a stronger position within a global system of White domination by distancing themselves from various racialised political categories, including, for example, Nativeness, Blackness, Asianness, and Muslimness. Education becomes a means of asserting this distance because it is where Whiteness is learned to be synonymous with civilisation, advancement, intelligence, wealth, progress, rationality, reason, and tolerance and racially subordinated groups with backwardness, irrationality, intolerance, poverty, and trauma. Education becomes a means of asserting this distance because institutions themselves can become racially coded as White or non-White. Education becomes a means of asserting this distance through under-resourcing and destroying educational systems and infrastructure that are associated with racially subordinated groups, exploiting the labour of racially subordinated groups, and extracting resources from former colonised regions of the world. Education becomes a means of asserting this distance, perhaps most forcefully, by actively denying the epistemic and material violence of this long and global history of White domination.

This theoretical observation has major implications for how it reorients education scholars and students to their areas of study and activism. For scholars focused on India, for example, this global critical race perspective might examine how education reproduces Hindu dominance by drawing on the racial and global positioning of Muslims as irrational and sub-rational and therefore unfit for nationhood or modernity. For scholars focused on China, this perspective might examine how education reproduces Han Chinese dominance by drawing on the global positioning of Black and Muslim people as unfit for nationhood or modernity. For scholars focused on Brazil, this perspective might examine how education reproduces White dominance through drawing on the global positioning of Black and Indigenous people as inferior and historically immature. For scholars focused on Israel and Palestine, this global critical race perspective might attend to how education has constructed Israel as an outpost of European civilisation and Whiteness—'the only democracy in the Middle East'—in relation to a construction of Palestinian people, and the Muslim political subject in particular, as unfit for modern nationhood. For environmental justice scholars, it provides a framework to establish links between the elimination of the natural world and the production of death-worlds (see Yusoff 2018). In each of the above examples, this orientation focuses attention on what is at stake on a global scale for those populations who are positioned as less proximate to Whiteness (or its complete lack). It is not merely oppression, segregation, and exclusion. The stakes are what they have always been in the modern/colonial world: the ongoing regulation, expulsion, and elimination of racially inferiorised and subordinated populations.

There is still much work to be done in developing this global critical race theory of education. One of the areas of focus that we did not delve into too deeply is how educational projects are implicated in the denationalisation of populations that are deemed to pose a threat to the purity of the modern nation-state. Through the Global War on Terror, countries throughout the world are expanding their powers to strip people of their citizenship and education must be operating as one site through which this stripping occurs and justification for this stripping is learned. This concern, in our view, is fundamentally a racial one. Another area of focus is how to approach intersectionality within a global critical race framework. In her global critical race perspective, Michelle Christian (2019, 182) has called for the integration of an intersectionality perspective into this approach. In decolonial thought, there has been a tendency to think of the racial cut between the European/White and racial and colonial Other as a structure that, as Ramón Grosfoguel (2011) put it, 'transversally reconfigures all of the other global power structures', including, for example, heteropatriarchy. This concept of *heterarchies* is akin to Patricia Hill Collins' (2009) concept of the matrix of domination. However, heterarchies foreground how this racial hierarchy in the modern/colonial world-system produces a single historical reality in the world we inhabit that, in turn, cuts across other power structures. This orientation may be useful in explaining and countering, for example, gendered Islamophobia from a transnational perspective. These are two areas that we intend to pursue moving forward.

While the global perspective outlined in this book takes a longer view of history and multi-scale approach to educational analyses than most approaches to critical race theory, the core commitment to racial emancipation endures. Indeed, decades after the introduction of critical race theory in educational studies, the challenge remains the same: forging models and systems of education that are racially emancipatory. An education for racial emancipation is not one that seeks to make individuals or institutional actors less racist. An education for racial emancipation seeks to dismantle the structures that enable racial violence in its various forms to endure. The structure that critical race theory has relentlessly challenged from its inception is the liberal nation-state. The liberal nation-state has an enduring racial problem, but so does the modern/colonial world. An education for global, racial emancipation is one that forges relations that do not wait for the unkept promises of modernity to be met. Around the world in the forgotten corners of neighbourhoods and nations, educators are already forging these models and systems of education each and every day. Their approaches are rooted in reciprocity not competition, collectivity not individualism, critique not complacency, potentiality not actualisation, interdependence not independence, redistribution not accumulation, generosity not possessiveness, generation not elimination. It is their efforts that give us hope that a better tomorrow is possible at a moment when the global order seems to be collapsing under its own conceits.

Other worlds are necessary.

Other worlds are possible.

References

Ali, Noor. 2022. 'Muscrit: Towards Carving a Niche in Critical Race Theory for the Muslim Educational Experience'. *International Journal of Research & Method in Education* 45 (4): 343–55. https://doi.org/10.1080/1743727X.2022.2103112.

Althusser, Louis. 1977. 'Ideology and Ideological State Apparatuses (Notes Toward an Investigation)'. In *Lenin and Philosophy and Other Essays*. Translated by Ben Brewster, Second, 119–73. London: NLB.

Annamma, Subini Ancy, David Connor, and Beth Ferri. 2013. 'Dis/Ability Critical Race Studies (DisCrit Theorizing at the Intersections of Race and Dis/Ability'. *Race Ethnicity and Education* 16 (1): 1–31. https://doi.org/10.1080/13613324.2012.730511.

Annovi, Claudia. 2023. 'P/CVE National Plans and Education as Strategy to Prevent Violent Extremism: The Case of France'. *International Review of Sociology* 33 (3): 388–402. https://doi.org/10.1080/03906701.2024.2322328.

Anyon, Jean. 1980. 'Social Class and the Hidden Curriculum of Work'. *The Journal of Education* 162 (1): 67–92.

Armstrong, Karen. 1992. 'The Andalus Legacy-A New World Discovered: An Old World Destroyed'. *European Judaism: A Journal for the New Europe* 25 (2): 3–11.

Balibar, Étienne. 1991. 'Is There a "Neo-Racism"?' In *Race, Nation, Class: Ambiguous Identities*, edited by Étienne Balibar and Immanuel Wallerstein, 17–29. Radical Thinkers. London: Verso.

© The Editor(s) (if applicable) and The Author(s) 2026
T. Denmead and A. Shareef, *Rethinking Critical Race Theory*, Palgrave Studies in Race, Inequality and Social Justice in Education,
https://doi.org/10.1007/978-3-032-07749-3

Bell, Derrick. 1980. 'Brown v. Board of Education and the Interest-Convergence Dilemma'. *Harvard Law Review* 93 (3): 518–533. https://doi.org/10.2307/1340546.

Bell, Derrick. 2018. *Faces at the Bottom of the Well: The Permanence of Racism.* New York: Basic Books.

Bigelow, Bill. 2024. 'School Curriculum Supports the Genocide. Here's How Teachers Can Push Back.' *These Times*, 7 October 2024. https://inthesetimes.com/article/teachers-school-curriculum-gaza-genocide.

Eduardo, Bonilla-Silva. 1997. 'Rethinking Racism: Toward a Structural Interpretation'. *American Sociological Review* 62 (3): 465. https://doi.org/10.2307/2657316.

Eduardo, Bonilla-Silva. 2010. *Racism without Racists: Color-Blind Racism and the Persistence of Racial Inequality in the United States*, 3rd ed. Lanham: Rowman & Littlefield Publishers.

Eduardo, Bonilla-Silva. 2012. 'The Invisible Weight of Whiteness: The Racial Grammar of Everyday Life in Contemporary America'. *Ethnic and Racial Studies* 35 (2): 173–194. https://doi.org/10.1080/01419870.2011.613997.

Eduardo, Bonilla-Silva. 2019. 'Feeling Race: Theorizing the Racial Economy of Emotions'. *American Sociological Review* 84 (1): 1–25. https://doi.org/10.1177/0003122418816958.

Eduardo, Bonilla-Silva. 2022. *Racism without Racists: Color-Blind Racism and the Persistence of Racial Inequality in America*, 6th ed. Lanham Boulder New York London: Rowman & Littlefield.

Brayboy, Bryan McKinley Jones. 2005. 'Toward a Tribal Critical Race Theory in Education'. *The Urban Review* 37 (5): 425–46. https://doi.org/10.1007/s11256-005-0018-y.

Breen, Damian. 2018. 'Critical Race Theory, Policy Rhetoric and Outcomes: The Case of Muslim Schools in Britain'. *Race Ethnicity and Education* 21 (1): 30–44. https://doi.org/10.1080/13613324.2016.1248828.

Browne, Simone. 2015. *Dark Matters: On the Surveillance of Blackness*. Durham, NC: Duke University Press.

Burchell, Graham, and Michel Foucault, eds. 2009. *The Foucault Effect: Studies in Governmentality*. Chicago, Ill: University of Chicago Press.

Busey, Christopher L., and Chonika Coleman-King. 2023. 'All Around the World Same Song: Transnational Anti-Black Racism and New (and Old) Directions for Critical Race Theory in Educational Research'. *Urban Education* 58 (6): 1327–1354. https://doi.org/10.1177/0042085920927770.

Christian, Michelle. 2019. 'A Global Critical Race and Racism Framework: Racial Entanglements and Deep and Malleable Whiteness'. *Sociology of Race and Ethnicity* 5 (2): 169–185. https://doi.org/10.1177/2332649218783220.

'Church of Saint Porphyrius Airstrike'. 2025. *Wikipedia.* https://en.wikipedia. org/w/index.php?title=Church_of_Saint_Porphyrius_airstrike&oldid=128739 0245.

Coppock, Vicki, and Mark McGovern. 2014. '"Dangerous Minds"? Deconstructing Counter-Terrorism Discourse, Radicalisation and the "Psychological Vulnerability" of Muslim Children and Young People in Britain'. *Children & Society* 28 (3): 242–256. https://doi.org/10.1111/chso.12060.

Corbin, Caroline Mala. 2017. 'Terrorists Are Always Muslim but Never White: At the Intersection of Critical Race Theory and Propaganda'. *Fordham Law Review* 86 (2).

Crenshaw, Kimberlé. 1991. 'Mapping the Margins: Intersectionality, Identity Politics, and Violence against Women of Color'. *Stanford Law Review* 43 (6): 1241–1299. https://doi.org/10.2307/1229039.

Crenshaw, Kimberlé, Neil Gotanda, Gary Peller, and Kendall Thomas. 1995. 'Introduction'. In *Critical Race Theory: The Key Writings That Formed the Movement*, edited by Kimberlé Crenshaw, Gary Peller, Neil Gotanda, and Kendall Thomas, xiii?xxxii. New York: New Press.

Crenshaw, Kimberle Williams. 2011. 'Twenty Years of Critical Race Theory: Looking Back to Move Forward'. *Connecticut Law Review* 43 (5): 1253–1353.

Dabashi, Hamid. 2019. 'The Incurable Parochialism of American Intellectuals'. *Al Jazeera.* 5 February 2019. https://www.aljazeera.com/opinions/2019/ 2/5/the-incurable-parochialism-of-american-intellectuals.

Dalrymple, Kelsey A., and Joel M. Phillips. 2024. 'The Complicated Rise of Social Emotional Learning in the United States: Implications for Contemporary Policy and Practice'. *Harvard Educational Review* 94 (3): 337–61. https://doi.org/10.17763/1943-5045-94.3.337.

Daulatzai, Sohail, and Junaid Akram Rana, eds. 2018. *With Stones in Our Hands: Writings on Muslims, Racism, and Empire. Muslim International.* Minneapolis: University of Minnesota Press.

Davidson, Miri. 2024. 'Decolonialism of the Far Right-Notes'. *E-Flux*, 24 May 2024. https://www.e-flux.com/notes/610730/decolonialism-of-the-far-right.

Davis, Mark. 2025. 'Violence as Method: The "White Replacement", "White Genocide", and "Eurabia" Conspiracy Theories and the Biopolitics of Networked Violence'. *Ethnic and Racial Studies* 48 (3): 426–446. https:// doi.org/10.1080/01419870.2024.2304640.

Delgado, Richard, and Jean Stefancic. 2023. *Critical Race Theory: An Introduction.* 4th ed. Critical America. New York: New York University Press.

Denmead, Tyler. 2021. 'Time after Whiteness: Performative Pedagogy and Temporal Subjectivities in Art Education'. *Studies in Art Education* 62 (2): 130–141. https://doi.org/10.1080/00393541.2021.1896252.

Denmead, Tyler, Amina Shareef and Duaa Karim. 2024. 'White Educability: Lessons from the Terror Trial of a Far-Right Nationalist in England'. *Discourse: Studies in the Cultural Politics of Education*, September, 1–12. https://doi.org/10.1080/01596306.2024.2396906.

Department for Education. 2023. 'Prevent Duty Guidance Update: A Briefing for Schools and Early Years Providers'. https://www.educateagainsthate.com/wp-content/uploads/2023/09/Prevent-Duty-Guidance-Schools-and-early-years-providers-briefing-note-1.pdf.

Douthat, Russ. 2025. 'The Anti-D.E.I. Crusader Who Wants to Dismantle the Department of Education'. *The New York Times*, March. https://www.nytimes.com/2025/03/07/opinion/chris-rufo-trump-anti-dei-education.html.

Dragoş, Simina. 2024. 'Towards a Decolonial and Anti-racist Analysis of the Nation-state and Nationalism'. *Sociology Compass* 18 (10): e70002. https://doi.org/10.1111/soc4.70002.

Drerup, Johannes. 2018. 'Education for Democratic Tolerance, Respect and the Limits of Political Liberalism'. *Journal of Philosophy of Education* 52 (3): 515–532. https://doi.org/10.1111/1467-9752.12337.

Du Bois W.E.B. 1940. *Dusk of Dawn*. The Oxford W.E.B. Du Bois. Oxford: Oxford University Press.

Du Bois W.E.B. 2008. *The Souls of Black Folk*. Edited by Brent Hayes Edwards. Reissued. Oxford World's Classics. Oxford: Oxford University Press.

Dussel Enrique. 2000. 'Europe, Modernity, Eurocentrism'. *Nepantla: Views from the South* 1 (3): 465?78.

Ellsworth, Elizabeth. 1989. 'Why Doesn't This Feel Empowering? Working through the Repressive Myths of Critical Pedagogy'. *Harvard Educational Review* 59 (3): 297–325.

Fanon, Frantz. 1965. *The Wretched of the Earth*. Translated by Constance Farrington. Grove: New York.

Fanon, Frantz. 2008. *Black Skin, White Masks*. Translated by Richard Philcox. New York: Grove Press.

Michel, Foucault. 1976. *Discipline and Punish: The Birth of the Prison*. New York: Random House.

Foucault Michel, and Colin Gordon. 1980. *Power/Knowledge: Selected Interviews and Other Writings, 1972–1977*. 1st American ed. New York: Pantheon Books.

Freeburg, Christopher. 2017. *Black Aesthetics and the Interior Life*. Charlottesville London: University of Virginia Press.

Freire, Paulo. 2000. *Pedagogy of the Oppressed*. 30th anniversary ed. New York: Continuum.

Gaztambide-Fernández, Rubén, Amelia M. Kraehe, and B. Stephen Carpenter II. 2018. 'The Arts as White Property: An Introduction to Race, Racism, and the Arts in Education'. In *The Palgrave Handbook of Race and the Arts in*

Education, edited by Amelia M. Kraehe, B. Stephen Carpenter II, and Rubén Gaztambide-Fernández, 1–32. Cham, Switzerland: Palgrave Macmillan.

Gillborn, David, Paul Warmington, and Sean Demack. 2023. *Quant: Crit An Antiracist Quantitative Approach to Educational Inquiry*. Place of publication not identified: Routledge.

Goldberg, David Theo. 2002. *The Racial State*. Malden, Mass: Blackwell Publishers.

Goldberg, David Theo. 2023. *The War on Critical Race Theory: Or, the Remaking of Racism*. Cambridge, UK; Hoboken, NJ: Polity.

Goodnight, Melissa Rae. 2017. 'Critical Race Theory in India: *Theory Translation* and the Analysis of Social Identities and Discrimination in Indian Schooling'. *Compare: A Journal of Comparative and International Education* 47 (5): 665–83. https://doi.org/10.1080/03057925.2016.1266926.

Grosfoguel, Ramón. (2011). Decolonizing Post-Colonial Studies and Paradigms of Political-Economy: Transmodernity, Decolonial Thinking, and Global Coloniality. *Transmodernity: Journal of Peripheral Cultural Production of the Luso-Hispanic World*, 1(1). https://doi.org/10.5070/T411000004

Grosfoguel, Ramón. 2012. 'Decolonizing Western Uni-Versalisms: Decolonial Pluri-Versalism from Aimé Césaire to the Zapatistas'. *Transmodernity: Journal of Peripheral Cultural Production of the Luso-Hispanic World* 1 (3). https://doi.org/10.5070/T413012884.

Grosfoguel, Ramón. 2013. 'The Structure of Knowledge in Westernized Universities Epistemic Racism/Sexism and the Four Genocides/Epistemicides of the Long 16th Century'. *Human Architecture: Journal of the Sociology of Self-Knowledge* XI (1): 73–90.

Grosfoguel, Ramón. 2016. 'What Is Racism' *Journal of World-Systems Research* 22 (1): 9–15. https://doi.org/10.5195/jwsr.2016.609.

Hall, Stuart, David Held, Don Hubert, and Kenneth Thompson, eds. 2011. *Modernity: An Introduction to Modern Societies*. Malden, Mass.: Blackwell.

Hall, Stuart and Media Education Foundation. 1996. 'Race the Floating Signifier'. Directed by Sut Jhally. Northampton, MA: Media Education Foundation.

Harpalani, Vinay. 2013. 'DesiCrit: Theorizing the Racial Ambiguity of South Asian Americans'. *NYU Annual Survey of American Law* 69: 77–184.

Harris, Cheryl. 1993. 'Whiteness as Property'. *Harvard Law Review* 106 (8): 1707–1791. https://doi.org/10.2307/1341787.

Heckman, James J., and Tim Kautz. 2012. 'Hard Evidence on Soft Skills'. *Labour Economics* 19 (4): 451–464. https://doi.org/10.1016/j.labeco.2012.05.014.

Hesse, Barnor. 2007. 'Racialized Modernity: An Analytics of White Mythologies'. *Ethnic and Racial Studies* 30 (4): 643–663. https://doi.org/10.1080/014 19870701356064.

Hill Collins, Patricia. 2009. *Black Feminist Thought: Knowledge, Consciousness, and the Politics of Empowerment*. 2nd ed. Routledge Classics. New York: Routledge.

HM Government. 2024. Prevent *Duty Guidance: For England and Wales*. https://www.gov.uk/government/publications/prevent-duty-guidance/pre vent-duty-guidance-for-england-and-wales-accessible.

Hochman, Adam. 2019. 'Racialization: A Defense of the Concept'. *Ethnic and Racial Studies* 42 (8): 1245–1262. https://doi.org/10.1080/01419870. 2018.1527937.

Holton, Woody. 2024. 'Chilling Affects'. *The American Historical Review* 129 (1): 199–216. https://doi.org/10.1093/ahr/rhae005.

Hooker, Juliet. 2017. 'Black Protest/White Grievance: On the Problem of White Political Imaginations Not Shaped by Loss'. *South Atlantic Quarterly* 116 (3): 483–504. https://doi.org/10.1215/00382876-3961450.

hooks, bell. 1992. 'Eating the Other: Desire and Resistance'. In *Black Looks: Race and Representation*, 21–39. Boston: South End Press.

'How to Identify Critical Race Theory'. n.d. The Heritage Foundation. Accessed 10 May 2025. https://www.heritage.org/civil-society/heritage-exp lains/how-identify-critical-race-theory.

Hussain, Adnan. 2022. 'Adnan Husain-About'. https://www.adnanhusain.org/ about.

Iftikar, Jon S., and Samuel D. Museus. 2018. 'On the Utility of Asian Critical (AsianCrit) Theory in the Field of Education'. *International Journal of Qualitative Studies in Education* 31 (10): 935–949. https://doi.org/10.1080/ 09518398.2018.1522008.

Inglis, David. 2011. 'Mapping Global Consciousness: Portuguese Imperialism and the Forging of Modern Global Sensibilities'. *Globalizations* 8 (5): 687–702. https://doi.org/10.1080/14747731.2011.617570.

James, C.L.R. 2001. *The Black Jacobins: Toussaint L'Ouverture and the San Domingo Revolution*, edited by James Walvin. New ed. London: Penguin.

Kattiparambil, Sheheen. 2024. 'Hindutva and the Muslim Subject'. *ReOrient* 8 (2). https://doi.org/10.13169/reorient.8.2.0142.

Katz, Mark. 2010. "What Exactly Is the 'War on Terror'" Middle East Policy Council. 30 September 2010. https://mepc.org/commentaries/what-exactly-war-terror/.

Kendi, Ibram X. 2019. *How to Be an Antiracist*. New York: One World.

Kennedy, Dane. 2016. Decolonization: A Very Short Introduction. *Oxford University Press*. https://doi.org/10.1093/actrade/9780199340491.001. 0001.

Kim, Sarang. 2022. 'A Transnational Application of Critical Race Theory: Schooling Experiences of Multicultural Students in South Korea'. *Multicultural Education Review* 14 (3): 194–208. https://doi.org/10.1080/200 5615X.2022.2129294.

King, Tiffany Lethabo. 2019. *The Black Shoals: Offshore Formations of Black and Native Studies.* Durham: Duke University Press.

Kliemann, Christiane. 2023. 'Contested Development Imaginaries: Hindutva and the Co-Optation of "Decolonisation"'. *Debating Development Research* (blog). 4 August 2023. https://www.developmentresearch.eu/?p=1596.

Kundnani, Arun. 2014. *The Muslims Are Coming! Islamophobia, Extremism, and the Domestic War on Terror.* London: Verso.

Ladson-Billings, Gloria, and William F. Tate IV. 1995. 'Toward a Critical Race Theory of Education'. *Teachers College Record* 97 (1): 47–68.

Leonhardt, David, Patrick Healy, and Jillian Weinberger. 2025. '"By the Time Trump Comes for Your University, It's Probably Too Late"'. *The New York Times*, 27 March 2025, Sec. Opinion. https://www.nytimes.com/2025/03/27/opinion/universities-trump-fight-back.html.

Lipsitz, George. 2006. *The Possessive Investment in Whiteness: How White People Profit from Identity Politics.* Philadelphia: Temple University Press.

Lowe, Lisa. 2015. *The Intimacies of Four Continents.* Durham: Duke University Press.

Maldonado-Torres, Nelson. 2007. 'On the Coloniality of Being'. *Cultural Studies* 21 (2–3): 240–270. https://doi.org/10.1080/095023806011 62548.

Maldonado-Torres, Nelson. 2017. 'The Decolonial Turn'. In *New Approaches to Latin American Studies.* Translated by Robert Cavooris. Routledge.

Matias, Cheryl E., Kara Mitchell Viesca, Dorothy F. Garrison-Wade, Madhavi Tandon, and Rene Galindo. 2014. '"What Is Critical Whiteness Doing in Our Nice Field like Critical Race Theory"' Applying CRT and CWS to Understand the White Imaginations of White Teacher Candidates?'. *Equity & Excellence in Education* 47 (3): 289–304.

Matsuda, Mari. 1995. 'Looking to the Bottom: Critical Legal Studies and Reparations'. In *Critical Race Theory: The Key Writings That Formed the Movement*, edited by Kimberlé Crenshaw, Neil Gotanda, Gary Peller, and Kendall Thomas, 63–79. The New Press.

Mbembe, Achille. 2003. 'Necropolitics'. *Public Culture* 15 (1): 11–40. https://doi.org/10.1215/08992363-15-1-11.

Mbembe, Achille. 2016. 'The Society of Enmity'. *Radical Philosophy*, 200: 23–35.

Meghji, Ali. 2021. 'Just What Is Critical Race Theory, and What Is It Doing in British Sociology' From "BritCrit" to the Racialized Social System Approach?.

The British Journal of Sociology 72 (2): 347–359. https://doi.org/10.1111/1468-4446.12801.

Meghji, Ali. 2022. 'Towards a Theoretical Synergy: Critical Race Theory and Decolonial Thought in Trumpamerica and Brexit Britain'. *Current Sociology* 70 (5): 647–664. https://doi.org/10.1177/0011392120969764.

Mesok, Elizabeth. 2022. 'Counterinsurgency, Community Participation, and the Preventing and Countering Violent Extremism Agenda in Kenya'. *Small Wars & Insurgencies* 33 (4–5): 720–741. https://doi.org/10.1080/09592318.2022.2037908.

Mesok, Elizabeth, and Darja Schildknecht. 2025. 'P/CVE-as-Counterinsurgency: Police Violence and Police Reform in Kenya's Counterterrorism Agenda'. *Security Dialogue*, February, 09670106241301672. https://doi.org/10.1177/09670106241301672.

Mielants, Eric, and Ramón Grosfoguel. 2006. 'The Long-Durée Entanglement between Islamophobia and Racism in the Modern/Colonial Capitalist/Patriarchal World-System'. *Human Architecture: Journal of the Sociology of SelfKnowledge* 5 (1): 1–12.

Mignolo, Walter D. 2000. *Local Histories/Global Designs: Coloniality, Subaltern Knowledges, and Border Thinking*. Princeton: Princeton University Press.

Miller, Daniel. 2018. 'Materiality: An Introduction'. UCL Anthropology. 10 July 2018. https://www.ucl.ac.uk/anthropology/people/academic-and-teaching-staff/daniel-miller/materiality-introduction.

Mills, Charles. 2007. 'White Ignorance'. In *Race and Epistemologies of Ignorance*, edited by Shannon Sullivan and Nancy Tuana, 13–38. SUNY Series, Philosophy and Race. Albany: State University of New York Press.

Misawa, Mitsunori. 2012. 'Social Justice Narrative Inquiry: A Queer Crit Perspective'. https://newprairiepress.org/aerc/2012/papers/34.

Modern World History: Patterns of Interaction. 1999. McDougal Littell / Houghton Mifflin.

Moore, Robert Ian. 1987. *The Formation of a Persecuting Society: Power and Deviance in Western Europe, 950–1250*. Oxford Cambridge (Mass.): Blackwell.

Mueller, Jennifer C. 2020. 'Racial Ideology or Racial Ignorance? An Alternative Theory of Racial Cognition'. *Sociological Theory* 38 (2): 142–169.

'Murder of Balbir Singh Sodhi'. 2025. *Wikipedia*. https://en.wikipedia.org/w/index.php?title=Murder_of_Balbir_Singh_Sodhi&oldid=1292113077.

Nash, Jennifer C. 2019. *Black Feminism Reimagined: After Intersectionality*. Durham, NC: Duke University Press.

Nelson, S. L. 2020. Towards a Transnational Critical Race Theory in Education: Proposing Critical Race Third World Approaches to Education Policy. *William and Mary Journal of Race, Gender, and Social Justice* 26 (5): 303–334.

Neocleous, Mark. 2011. 'The Police of Civilization: The War on Terror XE 'Global War on Terror' as Civilizing Offensive: The War on Terror as Civilizing Offensive'. *International Political Sociology* 5 (2): 144–159. https://doi.org/10.1111/j.1749-5687.2011.00126.x.

Newman, Edward, and Chi Zhang. 2021. 'The Mass Line Approach to Countering Violent Extremism in China: The Road from Propaganda to Hearts and Minds'. *Asian Security* 17 (2): 262–278. https://doi.org/10.1080/14799855.2020.1825379.

Nguyen, Mimi Thi. 2012. *The Gift of Freedom: War, Debt, and Other Refugee Passages*. Next Wave: New Directions in Women's Studies. Durham: Duke University Press.

Nguyen, Nicole. 2019. *Suspect Communities: Anti-Muslim Racism and the Domestic War on Terror*. Minneapolis: University of Minnesota Press.

Nguyen, Nicole. 2023. 'Mitigating or Exacerbating the Root Causes of Violence? Critically Analysing the Role of USAID in Terrorism Prevention'. *Conflict, Security & Development* 23 (5): 401–424. https://doi.org/10.1080/14678802.2023.2270434.

Niemi, Pia-Maria., Saija Benjamin, Arniika Kuusisto, and Liam Gearon. 2018. 'How and Why Education Counters Ideological Extremism in Finland'. *Religions* 9 (12): 420. https://doi.org/10.3390/rel9120420.

Nyong'o, T. (2009). *The amalgamation waltz: Race, Performance, and the Ruses of Memory*. Minneapolis: University of Minnesota Press.

Omi, Michael, and Howard Winant. 1994. *Racial Formation in the United States*. Second. New York: Routledge.

Pogue, James. 2022. 'Inside the New Right, Where Peter Thiel Is Placing His Biggest Bets'. *Vanity Fair*, 20 April 2022. https://www.vanityfair.com/news/2022/04/inside-the-new-right-where-peter-thiel-is-placing-his-biggest-bets.

Preventing Violent Extremism through Education: A Guide for Policy-Makers. 2017. Paris, France: United Nations Educational, Scientific and Cultural Organization.

Rana, Junaid Akram. 2011. *Terrifying Muslims: Race and Labor in the South Asian Diaspora*. Durham: Duke University Press.

Rathod, Bharat. 2022. *Dalit Academic Journeys: Stories of Caste, Exclusion and Assertion in Indian Higher Education*, 1st ed. London: Routledge India. https://doi.org/10.4324/9781003224822.

Razack, Sherene. 2022. *Nothing Has to Make Sense: Upholding White Supremacy Through Anti-Muslim Racism*. Muslim International. Minneapolis: University of Minnesota Press.

Reddy, Chandan. 2011. *Freedom with Violence: Race, Sexuality, and the US State*. Durham: Duke University Press.

Remensnyder, Amy G. 2017. 'The Boundaries of Christendom and Islam: Iberia and the Latin Levant'. In *The Oxford Handbook of Medieval Christianity*, edited by John Arnold, First published in paperback, 93–113. Oxford Handbooks. Oxford: Oxford University Press.

Sabir, Rizwaan. 2017. 'Blurred Lines and False Dichotomies: Integrating Counterinsurgency into the UK's Domestic "War on Terror."' *Critical Social Policy* 37 (2): 202–224. https://doi.org/10.1177/0261018316683471.

Said, Edward. 1975. *Beginnings: Intentions and Method*. London: Granta Books.

Said, Edward. 1978. *Orientalism*. New York: Pantheon Books.

Said, Edward. 2013. 'The Politics of Knowledge'. In *Race, Identity and Representation in Education*, edited by Cameron McCarthy, 2. ed., 453–60. Critical Social Thought.

Sayyid, S. 2014. *Recalling the Caliphate: Decolonisation and World Order*. London: C. Hurst.

Selod, Saher, and David G. Embrick. 2013. 'Racialization and Muslims: Situating the Muslim Experience in Race Scholarship'. *Sociology Compass* 7 (8): 644–655. https://doi.org/10.1111/soc4.12057.

Sexton, J. 2008. *Amalgamation schemes: Antiblackness and the critique of multiracialism*. Minneapolis: University of Minnesota Press.

Shahjahan, Riyad A., Annabelle L. Estera, Kristen L. Surla, and Kirsten T. Edwards. 2022. '"Decolonizing" Curriculum and Pedagogy: A Comparative Review Across Disciplines and Global Higher Education Contexts'. *Review of Educational Research* 92 (1): 73–113. https://doi.org/10.3102/003465432 11042423.

Shareef, Amina. 2023. *'Besieged Life'*. PhD, Cambridge: University of Cambridge.

Sirin, Selcuk R., and Michelle Fine. 2008. *Muslim American Youth: Understanding Hyphenated Identities through Multiple Methods*. Qualitative Studies in Psychology. New York: New York Univ. Press.

Solórzano, Daniel G. 1997. 'Images and Words That Wound: Critical Race Theory, Racial Stereotyping, and Teacher Education'. *Teacher Education Quarterly* 24 (3): 5–19.

Solórzano, Daniel G., and Tara J. Yosso. 2001. 'Critical Race and LatCrit Theory and Method: Counter-Storytelling'. *International Journal of Qualitative Studies in Education* 14 (4): 471–495. https://doi.org/10.1080/095 18390110063365.

Solórzano, Daniel G., and Tara J. Yosso. 2002. 'Critical Race Methodology: Counter-Storytelling as an Analytical Framework for Education Research'. *Qualitative Inquiry* 8 (1): 23–44. https://doi.org/10.1177/107780040200 800103.

Spivak, Guyatri. 1988. 'Can the Subaltern Speak?' In *Marxism and the Interpretation of Culture*, ed. Cary Nelson and Laurence Grossberg, 271–313. Urbana and Chicago: University of Illinois Press.

Sriprakash, Arathi, Sophie Rudolph, and Jessica Gerrard. 2022. *Learning Whiteness Education and the Settler Colonial State*. London: Pluto Press.

Stam, Robert, and Ella Habiba Shohat. 2012. *Race in Translation: Culture Wars around the Postcolonial Atlantic*. New York: New York University Press.

'Summer Programme-Critical Muslim Studies'. 2025. https://criticalmuslimstud ies.co.uk/summer-programme/.

Sweet, James H. 1997. 'The Iberian Roots of American Racist Thought'. *The William and Mary Quarterly* 54 (1): 143–166.

The United States Department of State and USAID. 2016. 'Joint Strategy on Countering Violent Extremism'. https://2009-2017.state.gov/documents/organization/257913.pdf.

Tuck, Eve, and K. Wayne Yang. 2012. 'Decolonization Is Not a Metaphor'. *Decolonization: Indigeneity, Education & Society* 1 (1): 1–40.

United Nations Human Rights Office of the High Commissioner. 2023. 'What You Need to Know about Preventing Violent Extremism Through Education'. 10 February 2023. https://www.unesco.org/en/articles/what-you-need-know-about-preventing-violent-extremism-through-education.

Viveros Vigoya, Mara. 2015. 'Social Mobility, Whiteness, and Whitening in Colombia'. *The Journal of Latin American and Caribbean Anthropology* 20 (3): 496–512. https://doi.org/10.1111/jlca.12176.

Wallerstein, Immanuel. 2004. World-Systems Analysis: An Introduction. *Duke University Press*. https://doi.org/10.1215/9780822399018.

Wang, Shuling, and Tyler Denmead. 2025. 'White Profitability: An Intersectional Critique of Chinese Women's Reckoning with the English Language Industry'. *Race Ethnicity and Education*, March, 1–21. https://doi.org/10.1080/13613324.2025.2474951.

Warmington, Paul. 2020. 'Critical Race Theory in England: Impact and Opposition'. *Identities* 27 (1): 20–37. https://doi.org/10.1080/1070289X.2019.1587907.

Watson Institute for International and Public Affairs. 2023. 'Human Costs of U.S. Post-9/11 Wars: Direct War Deaths in Major War Zones | Figures | Costs of War'. The Costs of War. August 2023. https://watson.brown.edu/costsofwar/figures/2021/WarDeathToll.

Weheliye, Alexander G. 2014. *Habeas Viscus: Racializing Assemblages, Biopolitics, and Black Feminist Theories of the Human*. Durham: Duke University Press.

Weinbaum, Alys Eve. 2019. *The Afterlife of Reproductive Slavery: Biocapitalism and Black Feminism's Philosophy of History*. Durham, NC: Duke University Press.

Weiner, Melissa F. 2012. 'Towards a Critical Global Race Theory'. *Sociology Compass* 6 (4): 332–350. https://doi.org/10.1111/j.1751-9020.2012.004 57.x.

Wimmer, Andreas, and Nina Glick Schiller. 2002. 'Methodological Nationalism and Beyond: Nation-State Building, Migration and the Social Sciences'. *Global Networks* 2 (4): 301–334. https://doi.org/10.1111/1471-0374.00043.

Wolfe, Patrick. 2006. 'Settler Colonialism and the Elimination of the Native'. *Journal of Genocide Research* 8 (4): 387–409. https://doi.org/10.1080/146 23520601056240.

World History. 2005. 2nd ed. Glencoe. New York, N.Y: Glencoe/McGraw-Hill.

Wynter, Sylvia. 1995. '1492: A New World View'. In *Race, Discourse, and the Origins of the Americas: A New World View*, edited by Vera Lawrence Hyatt and Rex Nettleford, 5–57. Washington, DC: Smithsonian Institution Press.

Wynter, Sylvia. 2003. 'Unsettling the Coloniality of Being/Power/Truth/ Freedom: Towards the Human, after Man, Its Overrepresentation-An Argument'. *CR: The New Centennial Review* 3 (3): 257–337.

Yao, Christina W., Chrystal A. George Mwangi, and Victoria K. Malaney Brown. 2019. 'Exploring the Intersection of Transnationalism and Critical Race Theory: A Critical Race Analysis of International Student Experiences in the United States'. *Race Ethnicity and Education* 22 (1): 38–58. https://doi. org/10.1080/13613324.2018.1497968.

Yeboah, Debbie. 2024. *'Healing the Colonial Wound: Decolonising Ghanaian Art Education through Reparative Art Praxis'*. Cambridge: University of Cambridge.

Yu, Min, Roland Sintos Coloma, Wenyang Sun, and Jungmin Kwon. 2024. 'Dissecting Anti-Asian Racism Through a Historical and Transnational AsianCrit Lens'. *Sociological Inquiry* 94 (2): 330–350. https://doi.org/10.1111/soin. 12572.

Yusoff, Kathryn. 2018. *A Billion Black Anthropocenes or None*. Forerunners: *Ideas First from the University of Minnesota Press 53*. Minneapolis: University of Minnesota Press.

Index

© The Editor(s) (if applicable) and The Author(s) 2026   113
T. Denmead and A. Shareef, *Rethinking Critical Race Theory*, Palgrave
Studies in Race, Inequality and Social Justice in Education,
https://doi.org/10.1007/978-3-032-07749-3

FSC
www.fsc.org
MIX
Papier | Fördert
gute Waldnutzung
FSC® C083411

Zeitfracht Medien GmbH
Ferdinand-Jühlke-Straße 7
99095 Erfurt, Deutschland
produktsicherheit@kolibri360.de